The Best Hill Walking in Scotland

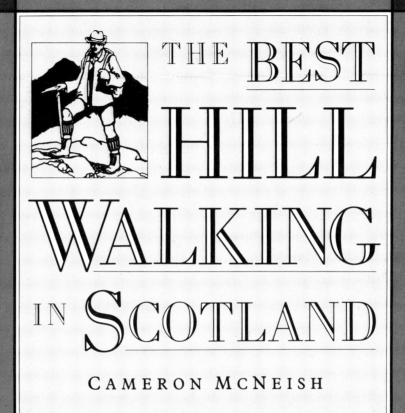

THE BEST HILL WALKING IN SCOTLAND

CAMERON MCNEISH

Neil Wilson Publishing•Glasgow•Scotland

Published by Neil Wilson Publishing
303a The Pentagon Centre
36 Washington Street
GLASGOW
G3 8AZ
Tel: 0141-221-1117
Fax: 0141-221-5363
E-mail: nwp@cqm.co.uk
http://www.nwp.co.uk/

A catalogue record for this book is available from the
British Library.

ISBN 1-897784-73-2

Designed by Hammond Hammond
Typeset in Plantin
Printed by SNP, Singapore

Introduction

SCOTLAND HAS SO much to offer the walker. It is a cornucopia which overflows with delights, offering everything from leisurely low-level forest walks to technical high-altitude expeditions demanding energy and stamina.

The variety of the land negates the possibility of boredom, and even the same place changes with the seasons. In choosing a number of 'best' walks, I am aware that I'm putting my head in a noose, for some will not agree with me. It's a no-win situation, but I don't care! The choice is mine, and these are some of my favourites. I say 'some' of my favourites because there are places in Scotland that I will never write about. They're too special to me, and probably for that reason they wouldn't be of any great interest to you, the reader.

'Best walks' are so often personal; fond memories and nostalgia are frequently the arbiters in such choices. Even a comparatively 'ordinary' walk can take on special proportions because of unchacteristically good weather, or because of the affability of one's companions.

Those familar with hill-walking in Scotland will recognise virtually all the walks I describe. I suppose that shows only that I'm little different from the thousands of walkers who tramp the hills every weekend; at the end of the day, most of us are attracted to roughly the same destinations, and those destinations take on the title of 'classics'. So, classic, best, favourite, most popular, or whatever, here they are, and I hope you too, come to consider them 'best', just as I have.

I have limited my choice to take in walks that can be enjoyed from six geographical centres, Ben Lomond and The Trossachs, Glen Coe, Lochaber, Torridon, Ullapool and Badenoch. In the awareness that many folk will come to holiday in Scotland for perhaps several days at a time, I felt it proper to encourage them to stay in one area for a while, and to enjoy the variety of walks there before moving on. So many people try to 'do' all of Scotland in a week, taking a bit here, a bite there, and invariably suffering acute indigestion because of it. Far better to enjoy a feast of Lochaber or Badenoch, and to come back next year and enjoy another area. That way you will come to know more of Scotland and its possibilities for walkers.

Using this method of listing walks allows me also to tell you more about each area, its history, its wildlife and its geography; and it allows you to realise that each area is unique and has certain qualities to offer that others don't possess.

Assuming reasonable weather, each area I have described should offer visitors a week of good walking discovering and enjoying the finest areas in Scotland.

Contents

Getting Around

SCOTLAND HAS PLENTY of public transport, except in the most remote areas, but even here the Postbus service can often take you where ordinary buses can't.

Scottish roads have been greatly improved over the past 30 years or so. Many of the once-infamous gradients and bends have been smoothed out and improved, and the motorway network in Central Scotland is complete, allowing rapid passage to the gateways to the Highlands of Stirling and Perth.

In the north, though, particularly the further north and west you go, many of the 'A' roads are still basically single-track roads with passing places. But they are generally well maintained and if you are happy to slow down and show some patience, you can actually enjoy the slower pace. One word about caravans: come high summer, the Highlands have two real pests – midges and caravans. Please be sure you can drive a car and caravan competently before heading off to the Highlands; and please consider the wisdom of towing a caravan on a single-track road. It really can make life hell for the locals. I honestly believe that caravan owners should have to take a test before they are allowed to venture out with caravan in tow. And we should have a law which bans caravans from being towed in convoy. Two or three car/caravan combinations makes life difficult indeed for someone wanting to get about his or her daily business. Please be considerate.

Scotland by Air

Scotland has direct services from European cities to Edinburgh, Glasgow, Prestwick, Inverness and Shetland. London flights are operated by **British Airways** and **British Midland** from Heathrow and by BA and **KLM UK** from Gatwick. **EasyJet** fly from Luton and both KLM UK and **Ryanair** fly out of Stansted.

The following numbers may be of use:

British Airways: 0345-222111
British Midland: 0345-554554

Scotland by Rail

Excellent rail services run from all parts of England to many Scottish towns and cities.

ScotRail services include links to Oban and Mallaig on the West Coast and via Inverness to Wick and Thurso in the North. ScotRail also operate the Caledonian Sleeper from London to Edinburgh, Glasgow, Aberdeen, Inverness and Fort William nightly, Sunday to Friday.

Getting Around (in 97) is published annually (with the relevant year in brackets) by ScotRail Marketing and copies are available from most Tourist Information Centres. This details all the relevant information on rail travel in Scotland. You can also call 0345 484950 for further information. **GNER** run trains into Edinburgh, Glasgow, Aberdeen and Inverness from London and other English cities en route and can be contacted on 0345 225225.

Scotland by Bus

Internal Scottish routes are run mainly by Scottish Citylink. The Trailpass offers unlimited travel throughout Britain for up to 15 days. Details from Scottish Citylink on 0990-505050.

Backpacker buses operate a jump on/jump off service around hostels and similar accommodation. Contact Go Blue Banana on 0131-556-2000, Haggis Backpackers on 0131-557-9393 and Mackbackpackers on 0131-220-1869.

Postbuses

Information on these important services is available from the Scottish Post Office Board, Operations Division (Postbuses), West Port House, West Port, Edinburgh, EH3 9HS. Contact 0131-228-7407. In Inverness the Postbus Controller can be contacted on 01463-256273.

Ferries

Major west-coast island links are provided by **Caledonian MacBrayne** who can be contacted on 01475-650100.

ACCOMMODATION

The tradition of Scottish hospitality is world-famous, and you will be assured of a warm welcome wherever you go in Scotland. Most towns and villages have hotels, guest-houses and plenty of bed-and-breakfast establishments. The Scottish Youth Hostels Association has about 80 hostels throughout the country, some in fine, remote spots. It's worth bearing in mind that you no longer have to be a 'youth' to use these facilities!

Scotland is still short of good, well-equipped campsites, but most villages have at least a field where you can park your caravan or pitch your tent for a few nights for a modest fee.

The Scottish Tourist Board, 23 Ravelston Terrace, Edinburgh EH4 3EU (0131-332-2433), publishes a useful range of publications and timetables, including *Where to Stay*, *What To Do* and *When Will You Go* and in conjunction with *The Great Outdoors*, also produces *Walk Scotland*.

Regional offices throughout Scotland can also give advance details of travel and accommodation. The STB website can be accessed on **www.holiday.scotland.net**.

THE MOUNTAIN CODE

▲ Respect private property and keep to paths when going through estates and farmland. Avoid climbing walls or fences and close any gate you have to open. Leave no litter.

▲ In the lambing season (March-May) and the stalking season (mid August-late October), enquire from local keepers, farmers or estate factors (or the police) before going on to the hills.

▲ In forests, keep to paths. Do not smoke or light fires. Avoid damaging young trees.

▲ Plan your route with care, taking into account the experience and fitness of all the party, and both prevailing and likely weather conditions. Allow plenty of time.

▲ Be properly equipped for the season, and take adequate food.

▲ Leave a note with a responsible person, giving

your route and likely time of return, and the names of the members of the party.

▲ Don't be afraid to turn back if conditions deteriorate or you find your expedition over-stretching you. There is always another day.

▲ Be particularly careful on descents, especially if the route is unfamiliar to you. If it easier to do so, go down by your route of ascent.

▲ In the event of an accident requiring a rescue team, one person should stay with the injured walker or climber while one or two go for help. If only two are in the party, the injured person should be left with all spare clothing and food while the other goes for help. To reach mountain rescue teams, dial, 999 and ask for the police.

WEATHER INFORMATION

The TGO Weathercheck can be accessed on the following basis (calls cost 50p/min at all times):
North-west Scotland 0891-112235
North-east Scotland 0891-112236
Central & Southern Scotland . . . 0891-112237

Gaelic Glossary

aber, abhair .... river's mouth, occasionally a confluence
achadh .... field, plain or meadow
aird .... height, high point, promontory
airidh .... sheiling, temporary shelter
allt .... river or stream
amhainn .... river
aonach .... ridge
ath .... ford

ban, bhan .... white, bright, fair
beag .... small
bealach .... pass, col or saddle
beith .... birch tree
ben, beinn .... hill or mountain
bidean .... peak
binnein .... peak
bodach .... old man
braigh .... brae, hill-top
breac .... speckled
brochan .... porridge
buachaille .... shepherd, herdsman, guardian
buidhe .... yellow
buiridh .... bellowing, roaring

cailleach .... old woman
camas .... bay
carn .... cairn, hill, pile of stones
cas .... steep
ceann .... head
choinneach .... mossy place, bog

chrois .... cross or crossing place
ciche .... pap, nipple
cill .... cell or church
cioch .... pap, nipple
ciste .... chest, coffin
clach .... stony
clachan .... small village, township
chap cnoc .... hillock
coille .... wood
coire, choire .... corrie, cwm
creachan .... rock
creag .... crag, cliff
croit .... croft
cruach, chruach .... hill
cuach .... cup, deep hollow
cul .... back
curra .... marsh, bog

dail .... field
damh, daimh .... stag
darach .... oakwood
dearg .... red, pink
diollaid .... saddle
diridh .... a divide
dorus .... strait, gate
drochaid .... bridge
drum, druim .... ridge
dubh .... dark, black
dun .... fort, stronghold
each .... horse
eagach .... notched place

eas .... waterfall
eighe .... file, notched
eileach .... rock
eilean .... island
eun .... bird

fada, fhada .... long
fearn .... alder
fiadh .... deer
fionn .... white
frith .... deer forest
fuar .... cold

gabhar .... goat
gaoth, gaoith .... wind
garbh .... rough
garbhanach .... rough ridge
gartain .... enclosed place
geal .... white
gearanach .... walled ridge
gearr .... short
gille .... young man, boy
glais .... burn
glas, ghlas .... grey or green
gleann .... glen
glomach .... chasm
gorm .... blue

innis, inch .... meadow, sometimes island
invir, inbhir .... confluence
iolair .... eagle

kin .... head
knock, cnoc .... hillock
kyle .... strait

ladhar .... forked, hooked
lagan, lag .... hollow
lairig .... pass
laoigh .... calf
laroch .... dwelling-place
leac .... stab, stone
leathad .... slope
leis .... lee, leeward
leitir .... slope
liath .... grey
lochan .... small loch

maighdean, mhaighdean .... maiden
mairg .... rust coloured
mam .... rounded hill
maol, mull .... headland, bare hill
meadhoin, mheadhoin .... middle
meall .... rounded hill
moin, mhoin, moine .... bog, or moss
monadh .... hill range, heathery hill
mor, mhor .... big
muc, muice .... pig
muilleann, mhuilinn .... mill
mullach .... top, summit

odhar .... dun-coloured
ord .... conical hill

poite .... pot
poll .... pool, pit
puist .... post

righ .... king

ros, ross .... promontory, moor
ruadh .... red
rubha, rudha .... point, promontory
ruigh .... sheiling

sail .... hell
sean, sin .... old
seileach .... willow
sgeir .... reef
sgiath .... wing
sgurr, sgorr .... sharp peak
sith .... fairy
sithean .... fairy hill
spidean .... peak
sron .... nose
stac .... steep rock, cliff, sea stack
steall .... waterfall
stob .... peak
stuc .... steep rock, peak
suidhe .... seat

tarmachan .... ptarmigan
teallach .... forge, hearth
tigh .... house
tir .... area, region, land
tobar .... well
tom .... hill
torr .... small hill
tulach, tulachan .... hillock

uaine .... green
uamh .... cave
uig .... bay
uisge .... water

1. Loch Lomond and The Trossachs

FOR GENERATIONS, LOCH Lomond and The Trossachs area has given a quiet relief to thousands of Clydesiders wishing to escape the hustle and bustle of their industrial environment. It is day-trip country, where, in summer, and especially at holiday weekends, the roads are crammed with cars and buses full of people admiring the countryside that equally enthralled such illustrious persons as Sir Walter Scott and William Wordsworth. Indeed, Scott once wrote:

O, Caledonia stern and wild,
Meek nurse for a poetic child,
Land of brown heath and shaggy wood,
Land of the mountain and the flood,
Land of my sires.

The Trossachs is well described as the 'Land of the mountain and the flood'. The area contains no fewer than 15 lochs, Scotland's lake district, most of them hemmed in by rugged, tree-clad mountains, not particularly high, but friendly and intimate. Lacking the stark barren-ness of the more northern hills, the area offers the walker a subtle combination of mountain, forest and loch scenery, with a wide variety of footpaths and forest trials.

Despite the number of trippers on the roads, and the fact that two of the lochs, Loch Arklet and Loch Katrine, have been commandeered by Strathclyde Regional Council to satisfy the thirsts of the citizenry of Glasgow and its surrounds, the area has lost little of its charm since the days of Scott and Wordsworth.

Once away from the roads and picnic spots, The Trossachs is a remarkably quiet area. In all my wanders in these hills, I can't remember coming across a lot of people at any one time, other than on one or two of the more popular routes, and, of course, on the West Highland Way, which runs up the east shore of Loch Lomond.

Autumn is the finest time to visit the area. It is then that the leaves on the trees, the multitude of oak and birch, are losing their bright greenery, turning gold and bronze as the season progresses, until they all turn red in a final gesture of flamboyance before submitting to the cruel hand of winter.

FAMOUS LOCHS

Loch Lomond is probably the best-known and most-revered of all Scotland's lochs. Lying on the western edge of the Highland Line, the geological fault which runs between Helensburgh in the west and Stonehaven in the east, it stands astride the Highlands and the Lowlands. Indeed, the spectacle is best admired from the top of Duncryne Hill, a small, dumpy hill which dominates the village of Gartocharn on the southern shore of the loch. From the hill's summit the grandeur of the Highlands is set before you in panoramic splendour. Almost beneath your feet are the green agricultural flats of the Lowlands; in front, the dark, island-studded waters of the loch, stretching into the distance, gradually being choked by higher and higher mountains until the sky away in front of you is a solid wall of jagged peaks.

DISTANT VIEWS

Almost as good a view can be enjoyed from Conic Hill, near Balmaha, on the banks of Loch Lomond itself, a much-more accessible hill than Duncryne. This hill actually straddles the Highland Line, and to the south you can actually see the skyscrapers of modern Glasgow. In front of you lies the Firth of Clyde and the jagged peaks of the Isle of Arran; to the north, the swell of the mountains, rising higher to the guardian hills of Ben Vorlich and Ben Vane.

For the ornithologist, these southern shores of Loch Lomond are wonderful. It's here that the summer migrants breed, the oyster-catchers, terns, dunlin, redshank, lapwings, plover, snipe and woodcock. Greenshank and wagtails pass by in the spring on their way north, and the flats are alive with the sound of curlew, mallard, tufted duck, moorhen and gulls.

The loch's islands, clad in oak, rowan, alder and pine, would make an excellent setting for a canoe trip. Clairinch has the remains of a *crannog*, an ancient lake-dwelling, and Inchcailloch houses the remains of a twelfth-century nunnery dedicated to St Kentigern's widow. Inchcailloch means Isle of the Old Woman.

As Loch Lomond dominates the surrounding

THE COBBLER, one of the finest 'wee mountains' in Scotland. What it lacks in height it gains in sheer personality. Many hillwalkers have been quoted as saying that they would gladly swap a hundred Munros for the Cobbler.

scenery, the loch is in turn dominated by Ben Lomond, the Beacon Hill. This is the first 3,000 ft peak that the north-bound traveller meets in Scotland. Rather big and bulky for poetic descriptions when viewed from the west bank of Loch Lomond, it rises up into a fine peak when viewed from the north.

From the summit of Ben Lomond, looking roughly north-east, lies a wild-looking area, though certainly not as sterile and barren as other areas of Scotland. Although the hills that surround Ben Lomond are considerably less in height than their northern cousins, they are certainly no less in character. Great corries bite into the hillsides, craggy bluffs and deeply-wooded ravines line the slopes, and tumbling cascades of stone and scree show where rushing streams have created fissures in the steep mountainsides, Long, winding promontories, like great roots, flow down and disappear into the lapping waters of the lochs. Birch, oak, ash and pine decorate the shores and the lower slopes, and here and there great, craggy upthrusts of rock burst from the foliage like ancient, craggy sentinels.

WILD ANCESTORS

If the area is wild, then its occupants in those far-off days of history were even wilder. Straddling the Highland Line, the clans to the north were, even until comparatively recently, as Scott so succinctly puts it, 'much addicted to predatory excursions upon their Lowland neighbours'. Although The Trossachs are situated on the edge of this line, a border country almost, it was virtually sequestered from the world, and, as it were, insulated with respect by society. Graham's *Sketches of Scenery in Perthshire* published in 1806, explains: 'Tis well known, that in the Highlands, it was in former times, accounted not only lawful, but honourable, among hostile tribes, to commit depradations on one another; and these habits of the age were perhaps strengthened in this district by the cir-cumstances which have been mentioned. It bordered on a country, the inhabitants of which, while they were richer, were less warlike than they, and widely differenced by language and manners'.

ROB ROY

All this is Macgregor territory. Their illustrious clan chief, Rob Roy Macgregor Campbell (he adopted the last name when his own clan name was proscribed), was born in a little house at the head of Loch Katrine. The area abounds with legends of him and his followers. History has painted him as something of a Scots Robin Hood, and the man was undoubtedly a character. A well-educated man, nature had endowed him with an abnormally long pair of arms with which, it is said, he could tie his garters without stooping! This also gave him a longer reach than anyone else, which made him something of an expert with the claymore, as many of his opponents found to their cost.

Rob Roy was Christened Robert, son of Lieut-Colonel Donald Macgregor, an officer in the army of Charles II, and Margaret Campbell, half-sister to the later-despised Campbell of Glenlyon, who was involved in the carrying out of the fateful orders which resulted in the infamous Massacre of Glen Coe in 1692. As the name Macgregor was proscribed at the time of Rob's birth, the local minister refused to cary out the christening ceremony, and Donald had to carry the child to the adjoining parish of Buchanan.

The Macgregors were incorrigible cattle-thieves and their complete flaunting of the laws of the day had come to a climax in 1603, when they slaughtered nearly 300 Colquhouns in a battle in Glen Fruin, and then went on to plunder the Colquhoun's land, near Luss. Almost immediately, Colquhoun himself led 220 widows to King James VI in Stirling. The mourning women carried in their arms the blood-splattered clothes of their dead husbands. The outcome was proscription of the name Macgregor, and total forfeiture of all the clan's lands. Outlawed, many of the men took to the hills, but continued in their plundering ways.

During the Jacobite uprisings, Rob Roy ironically supported the Stewart cause and fought in the Battle of Sherrifmuir. The guerilla tactics which he and his followers employed in both thieving and battle, added to the fact that according to the law they were nameless, brought them the nickname of Children of the Mist.

Despite Rob Roy's fiery life, he lived to a good age and died peacefully in his own bed. His grave, and that of his wife, Helen Campbell, are in the tiny churchyard at Balquidder, on the shore of Loch Voil.

A long backpacking route that takes in much of the splendour of The Trossachs begins at Ardui, on the A82 Glasgow to Fort William road. There is also a railway station. The first two miles of this route follows the main road north to the footbridge over the River Falloch, just north of Inverarnon. As you cross the bridge, you'll see a magnificent view of the Beinglas Waterfall, where

F ERAL GOATS on the slopes of Ben Lomond. You'll probably smell them before you see them. It is thought these goats are descended from Persian white goats which were kept many years ago. Only a few areas are left in Scotland where feral goats can be seen.

the waters cascade down a cliff on the hillside. Passing the foot of the waterfall, a path leads south, the route of the busy West Highland Way, towards the Dubh Lochan and on past Doune to Inversnaid.

Continue south and you are on one of the finest sections of the West Highland Way, if one of the busiest. This used to be a delightful stretch before the designation of 'official' long-distance footpath status. Now, heavy usage has taken away the 'wilderness feel to this side of Loch Lonmond. But you can still enjoy it, crossing the many green meadows and rocky ravines flecked with natural woodland and giving fine views across the loch towards The Cobbler and Ben Narnain, two of the Arrochar Alps. Watch out for red deer and feral goats.

Many years ago, John Groome, who lived in the remote house at Caillness, put up some signs urging walkers to beware of the haggis-shooting season. John was a good friend to walkers and ramblers and would often invite them to join him for a 'cuppa'. Sadly, he was forced to leave Caillness and move to Cartocharn, and a new landowner locked up the house, which is now in a sad state of repair. An ugly, bulldozed track runs up the hillside behind the house, marring what was once an idyllic spot.

Continue on the path to Rowardennan, and then climb Ben Lomond by way of the Sron Aonach ridge. From the summit, retrace your steps a little way to skirt the north-east cliffs of the Coire a Bhathaich and descend the steep slopes to the steading called Comer. From here a track leads down to the road at Kinlochard. Follow the road for a mile to just before another hotel, where a right-of-way climbs north beside the Ledard

Burn. Below Beinn Bhreac, the path swings north-east and leads up to the 2,386 ft summit of Ben Venue.

You are now in the very heart of The Trossachs, with Loch Katrine and Loch Achray seemingly at your feet. Descend now, down steep heather-covered slopes, and on to the Forestry Commission road which runs along the north shore of Loch Katrine. Continue on the track to the end of the loch, and past Rob Roy's old house at the entrance to Glen Gyle. At the head of Glen Gyle lie the craggy slopes of Ben Ducteach, whose north-east slopes should be skirted before you go over the saddle to the Beinn Glas burn again. Descend the slopes, steep in places, taking a closer look at the Grey Mare's Tail, and drop down to Beinglas Bridge and the two-mile walk back to Ardlui. The total distance walked is about 48 miles. With plenty of hotel accommodation to choose from, it makes a good long-weekend expedition.

FOREST WALKS

A shorter trip in similar vein begins at a little hamlet called Brig o'Turk, situated on the A821 road between Callander and Aberfoyle. Begin by taking the minor road north from Brig o'Turk to the reservoir in Glen Finglas, and then through the Bealach a Chonnaidh to Balquidder. Leave the village on the south side of the River Balvaig and take the minor road to Strathyre. Continue through Strathyre until you reach a footpath on the west shore of Loch Lubnaig. Follow this path for about four miles until the Forestry houses at Stank are reached, where a Forestry track and footpath leads up into the Stank Glen, a big, open corrie just below the summit slopes of Ben Ledi.

Take time to explore the fine pinnacles on the south side of the glen. Climb to the summit of Ledi and descend due west, down easy slopes to Gleann Casaig and Glen Finglas reservoir again. This is a good two-day walk of 24 miles.

The area offers a multitude of loch-side and forest walks, with the huge Queen Elizabeth Forest Park opening up miles of forest track. Aberfoyle, Ardlui, Callander and Kinlochard are all good centres for exploring in these hills and lochs, and for walkers who enjoy a spot of angling in the evening, opportunities abound.

Away from the tourist spots, these hills are wild and quiet. The naturalist will find plenty to challenge his skill, and the romantic may well enjoy following the writings of Sir Walter Scott. The Children of the Mist may well be long gone, but they have left behind a wealth of history and legend, some perhaps glorified and exaggerated, but neverthless leaving The Trossachs the richer for it.

Ben Lomond, Trossachs and Loch Lomond

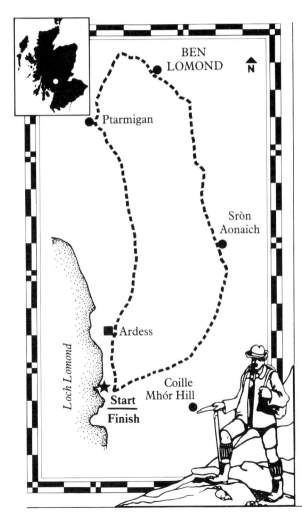

MAP: Ordnance Survey Sheet 56.

DISTANCE: Seven miles.

ASCENT: 3,000 ft.

DIFFICULTIES: No real problems as a path runs all the way to the summit. Care is needed in winter and spring, though, when snow covers the path and some slopes may be slippy. Much of the path tends to be muddy in the wetter conditions of higher summer.

ACCOMMODATION: Youth hostel at Rowardennan. Camp-sites along the east shore of Loch Lomond between Balmaha and Rowardennan. Hotels, guest-houses and bed-and-breakfast at Balloch, Balmaha, Drymen and Gartocharn.

Bonny Ben Lomond is a Glaswegian's hill. Mention 'The Ben' to a citizen of that great city and his heart will take him to the wooded shores of Loch Lomond and the Beacon Hill that dominates it. Most other people will think of Ben Nevis, *the* Ben in terms of height alone.

On a good day you can see Ben Lomond from some of the high points in the city. An hour-and-a-half drive from Stirling will take you to its foot. The most southerly of all Scotland's Munros, it straddles the Highland Boundary Fault which runs from Helensburgh to Stonehaven, near Aberdeen. As such, it forms a dividing line between Highland and Lowland Scotland, a division which is both abrupt and dramatic.

My last visit to Ben Lomond was dramatic in itself. The summit was well-doused by a swathe of grey cloud, and the burns and streams coursed down the flanks with urgency and impatience. On the lochside, by the car-park at Rowardennan, the start of the walk, the wind whipped through the trees, those grand ancient oaks and the more modern larches and spruces, and the surface of the loch boiled and fumed with wave and spray.

Ben Lomond is owned by the National Trust for Scotland, which has done some work on the footpath which runs up the broad whaleback to the summit. A signpost points out the route opposite the Rowardennan Hotel. The path takes you quickly up over the lower slopes, past birch- and oak-woods and through dense thickets of bracken. Away to your left, provided it isn't misty, the summit sits squatly atop its broad shoulders. The summit is, in fact, a fine curved ridge about half-a-mile long, from which sheer cliffs fall to the north and east.

ANCIENT TREES

Wander up the path and enjoy the sight of island-studded Loch Lomond opening up behind you. This is the largest sheet of inland water in the country, and arguably the most beautiful. Certainly that claim to fame is enhanced by the remarkable combination of water, mountain and woodland, a combination that is almost unique in such scale in Scotland. And, thankfully, the trees are not all imported spruce, but ancient natural broadleaves, oak, birch, chestnut and beech.

Another characteristic of Loch Lomond is that

THE SUMMIT of Ben Lomond from the Arrochar Alps, separated by the gulf of Loch Lomond. It's well seen why Ben Lomond was named the Beacon hill. It is also the most southerly of all Scotland's 3000 foot mountains.

while its feet are firmly embedded in the Lowlands, its head and shoulders are choked by Highland mountains. As you climb up on to the broad, whalebacked shoulder of Ben Lomond, look south and admire the Lowland view, low volcanic hills rolling into the industrial haze of Clydeside. On good days you'll see the ragged outline of the Isle of Arran in the Firth of Clyde, and perhaps even the Ailsa Craig, known as Paddy's Milestone, and said to be halfway between Scotland and Ireland.

SUMMIT RIDGE

Continue north, off the broad shoulder and on to the path which traverses across the steeper summit slopes. To your right the hills and lochs of The Trossachs will be coming into view, and to your left the sharp outline of the Arrochar Alps dominate the view, The Cobbler, Ben Narnain, Ben Vane and Ben Vorlich.

The path soon tops out on the summit ridge, a well-worn and obvious path which carries you around the rim of the northern corries which fall away to Comer, far below, and the silver burn which is the infant River Forth.

Here, on the summit, you have a choice. You can either descend by the way you came, or carry on northwards, and then west, by a well-worn path which takes you down onto the Ptarmigan Ridge of the hill which will carry you down to Rowardennan. I strongly recommend the latter, for it takes you into an area above the true heart of the hill, the rocky slopes that stretch down to the magic seclusion of the Cailness Corrie, the haunt of red deer, wild goats and eagle.

The Ptarmigan Ridge offers a fine descent line, and on the day I mentioned earlier I had to

A ROARING waterfall on the Ptarmigan Ridge of Ben Lomond. This area gets its fair share of rain and after a heavy spell of weather the waterfalls come into their own.

navigate through thick cloud to find it. But as I came below the cloud level, the grey outline of Loch Lomond stretched northwards, with a thin and watery silvery sunbeam glistening on it. The east bank looked really wild and lonely from here, a stark contrast to the busy A82 road on the opposite bank. A ridge of hinds stopped me in my tracks as I came from below the cloud, the greyness and thin mist exaggerating their outline. There was a mystical quality in the light, the half-light melted the foreground and the deer looked as though they were floating on cloud. And then, in a

flick of an eye, they were gone.

The return to Rowardennan down the ridge was a treat. The archipelago of islands at the south end of the loch lit up as beams of silvery sunlight burst through the dark cloud. And despite the greyness, there was still colour around. Muted in November garb it may have been, but the blond of the deer grass was still vivid, as were the reds and ochres of the dead bracken. Only the birches were devoid of leaf, but their skeletal copper tinge added the final touch to the scene.

The Cobbler, Loch Lomond and The Trossachs

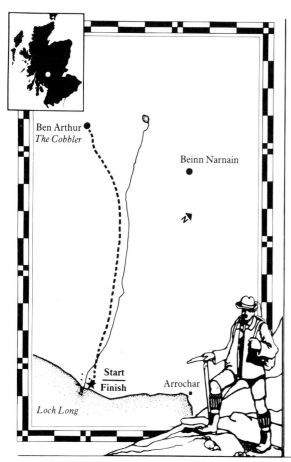

Ben Arthur
The Cobbler

Beinn Narnain

Start
Finish

Arrochar

Loch Long

MAP: Ordnance Survey Sheet 56.

DISTANCE: Five miles.

ASCENT: 2,500 ft.

DIFFICULTIES: An easy and straightforward hill-walk. The Central Peak, the real summit, involves some scrambling which certainly won't be everyone's cup of tea, but The Cobbler gives a great day out whether you scramble the final few feet or not.

ACCOMMODATION: Youth hostels at Ardgarten and Crianlarich. Hotels, guest-houses and bed-and-breakfast in Arrochar, Tarbet and Crianlarich.

It's odd how we often consider mountains in an anthropological sense. We give them characters, and moods and more often than not we treat them as something with which we do battle. The military metaphor in mountaineering literature is commonplace. Some mountains make us feel wary, on guard, while others seem gentler, infinitely more benign. A chance encounter with a small dog on my very first visit to The Cobbler shaped my feelings towards this hill in a very real way.

I was walking up beside the Buttermilk Burn on a day of thick mist when a little black-and-white collie appeared beside me. He was a jolly character, boisterous and wagging his tail. I waited a while, for I was sure his owner would appear on the path beside me, but after waiting, then whistling and shouting, it seemed to me that the dog was on his own. He seemed quite happy to follow me, and he did, all the way to the summit, where he cheekily scoffed most of my sandwiches.

FULL OF CHARACTER

I must admit that I thoroughly enjoyed the little fellow's company. He really was a delight, full of cheek, and very sure of himself. The notion even entered my head that I could take him to the Police Office in Arrochar and, if no-one claimed him, take him home. But, strangely, when I think of it now, when we reached the spot where he first picked me up, he vanished. One moment he was beside me, the next he was gone, back into the mist whence he came.

Now I'm not for one moment claiming that this little character was a canine spectre; ghosts don't 'wolf' down your sandwiches and piss up against your rucksack as this lad did. But I rather liked the notion that this wee dog was like the very 'persona' of The Cobbler, cheeky, a bit cocky and sure of himself, and good company.

The Cobbler's just like that, small and different, with all the attributes of much bigger hills (and many attributes lacking in bigger hills),

THE COBBLER, or Ben Arthur, in winter raiment. Although small in stature, the Cobbler can be a formidable hill in winter. Cornices have been known to form along the summit ridge and avalanches have been known to occur from time to time.

THE SOUTH Peak of the Cobbler – sometimes known as the Cobbler's wife. This summit is the most difficult to climb. The North summit is the easiest while the middle summit, the highest point on the hill, requires some scrambling and a cool head.

and it gives this impression of being a bit cheeky. I would rate it among my top five favourites in the country.

It's almost an indication of the affection people have for this hill that it's best known, and generally referred to, by its nickname. Its real name is Ben Arthur, and it stands 2,891 ft above sea level. It's also an incredibly rocky mountain, possibly the only hill of its height in the country that requires the skills of a rock-climber to get you on the summit. The final few feet have caused many a cheery rambler to turn back, which is a shame, because it's not really all that difficult. Like so many of these situations, it looks worse than it is.

TRIPLE-TOPPED

I first set eyes on The Cobbler when I climbed Ben Lomond for the first time as a raw schoolboy. I was impressed by the surreal attitude of this odd-shaped mountain away across the gulf formed by Loch Lomond. Triple-topped and oddly prehistoric, it dominated the other, bigger, hills known collectively as the Arrochar Alps. It's this odd shape that gives The Cobbler its nickname, because some suggest that it resembles a cobbler at his last. It has three distinct summits, the left one formed into a leaning pyramid, the Central Peak, the true summit, appearing as a flat-topped table, while the North Peak is an immense overhanging prow, a remarkable feature which boasts many of the mountain's best rock-climbs.

The most popular route to The Cobbler is by Arrochar, which straggles around the head of Loch Long. Like many other villages in this area, and further south by Gareloch and Faslane, Arrochar suffers from the over-presence of the MOD. In fact, this walk begins on the Arrochar road, just opposite the old torpedo-testing station, where the Buttermilk Burn enters Loch Long.

SHEER DROPS

A good path runs up through the woods close by the stream, and soon breaks free of the trees and on to the open moorland above, where you'll get your first glimpse of the mountain. The most straightfoward route to the top is by the obvious *bealach* between the North and Central Peaks of the hill. Cross the Buttermilk Burn on to its east bank, and follow the broad, muddy path on past the Narnain Boulders (one of them forms an overhanging shelter, a good 'howff' on a bad day).

As you approach the hill, enthralled, no doubt, by its rocky verticalities, you'll have to cross the burn again and make your way up into the rock-strewn corrie. Rock dominates. Climb steeply up below the overhanging face of the North Peak, and on to the gentle *bealach*. Turn right and follow the well-worn path that leads to the flat top of the North Peak. Take care for the drops are sheer on three sides – and enjoy the views. Ben Lomond dominates the views to the south, and closer at hand the other Arrochar Alps rise in sharp relief. Across the glen, Ben Narnain and Beinn Ime are particularly impressive, and across the corrie the crags of the Central Peak rise high above the long, sinuous arm of Loch Long.

Make your way down to the *bealach* again and along the ridge towards the Central Peak. The route to the summit isn't too evident, but you'll see a narrow window in the rock above you. This is where you wish you could lose half-a-stone in weight, or bulk, because you have to squeeze through here, through this eye of a needle.

Beyond the slit, you'll find yourself on a narrow ledge which traverses off to the left. Follow this around the back of the rock to where a couple of easy holds carry you on to the summit platform. The exhilaration is dynamic!

The South peak isn't really for walkers and involves a bit more than scrambling to reach its summit.

Ben Venue, The Trossachs and Loch Lomond

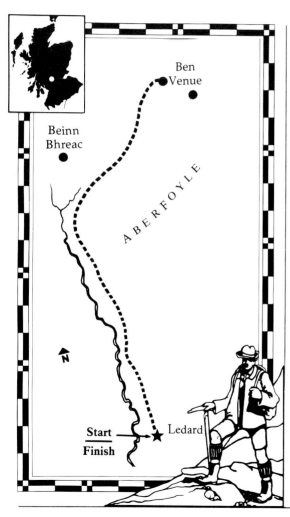

MAP: Ordnance Survey Sheet 57.

DISTANCE: Nine miles to the summit and back.

ASCENT: 2,100 ft.

DIFFICULTIES: A straightforward walk on a good path all the way. No real difficulties.

ACCOMMODATION: Hotels, guest-houses and bed-and-breakfast in Aberfoyle and Callander.

'I want to go climb a hill where there's a good view, some good legends, and which isn't a mountaineering expedition'. So said my friend, Peter, home in Scotland for Christmas and with a surfeit of energy. Years of soft-living in the States had given him that identifiable pear-shape, so I guessed it would have to be a pretty easy hill. I chose Ben Venue, in The Trossachs.

Ben Venue, Hill of the Caves, is one of the finest 'wee hills' in the southern Highlands. With its twin tops, its western outliers, and its rugged countenance, it lords over the craggy landscape of The Trossachs, and yet is an easy-enough hill to climb. The slopes which tumble down towards the shores of Loch Katrine contain the Bealach nam Bo, the Pass of the Cattle, a trade route in centuries past for cattle going to the Falkirk Tryst and a backdoor for beasts stolen by the Clan MacGregor.

Close by is Coire na Urisgean, or the Corrie of the Goblins. Sir Walter Scott, who roamed this area and found inspiration for his works, depicted the Goblin's Corrie as a retreat for Ellen Douglas and her father after they had withdrawn from Roderick Dhu's stronghold on an island on Loch Katrine.

Rather than tackle the hill head-on, over and up its cragg bluffs, from the east-facing Trossachs side, we drove over the Duke's Pass to Aberfoyle, along Loch Ard-side and parked the car near Ledard. A footpath sign points the way, proclaiming that it is seven miles to The Trossachs via the summit of Ben Venue.

This is a good route up the hill. The ascent is longer, but climbs at a conveniently easy and steady gradient, just the thing for my overweight friend. We passed the Ledard Farm, where Cashmere goats are bred and farmed.

IMPRESSIVE VIEWS

I wondered what Scott would have thought of it. He stayed at this very building, where he worked on his notes for *Rob Roy* and *Waverley*. Indeed, behind the farm and close by the footpath, is a fine waterfall and pool where Scott apparently wrote when the weather was good.

The path takes an obvious line alongside the Ledard Burn, and eventually carries you high on to the eastern slopes of one of Venue's outliers, Beinn Bhreac. Here, a wide *bealach* takes you on to the craggy slopes of Ben Venue, and the first views of the day start to impress.

Away to the west, Loch Katrine stretches, one of its ancient arms cut off now by the strip of land at Stronachlachar. Loch Arklet forms that old arm, running in a transverse line towards the deep trench that holds Loch Lomond. To the north, the Crianlarich hills bow their heads to the higher tops of Stobinian and Ben More, and further east the Ben Lawers range all but dwarf the neighbouring Tarmachans. It's tremendous scenery in all directions.

By the time we reached the summit ridge, Peter was beginning to tire, but heartily agreed that the walk was hardly a mountaineering expedition. He was delighted with the views, which now stretched as far as the eye could see. Mountains were everywhere, but they paled into insignificance compared to the countryside closer at hand. The long lochs of The Trossachs were like elongated pools of quicksilver in the afternoon light, and below, the emerald forest and the rust-coloured hue of the birchwoods wove a delightful tapestry against a background of snow-tinged hills.

EVOCATIVE LEGENDS

The walk was good, the views were fine; now I needed only a legend to keep my part of the bargain. As we sat by the summit cairn, eating our piece, I took out of my pack a well-thumbed copy of Scott's *Lady of the Lake*. I read aloud the verses about the end of the stag-chase at the foot of Ben Venue . . .

It is late in the day and the sun is sinking beyond the western horizon. The knight is left alone. His horse, exhausted from the chase, dies quietly and the hounds are recalled. When the echoes of the horn fade away, the beauties of the hollows, the woods and the hills are magnificently described. It is brilliant, evocative writing. I pause for effect, and glance up to see if Peter is enjoying it.

He has fallen asleep – his great pear-shaped body wedged up against the summit cairn, head on chest, oblivious to the romantic brilliance of one of Scotland's greatest bards. You can't win them all . . .

Ben A'An, The Trossachs and Loch Lomond

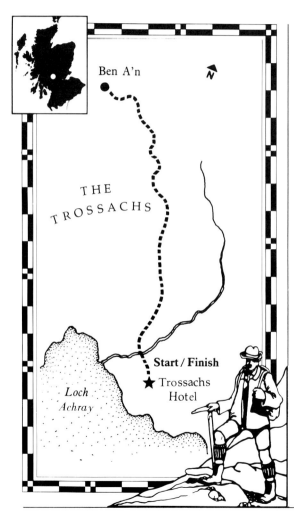

MAP: Ordnance Survey Sheet 56.

DISTANCE: Four miles.

ASCENT: 1,200 ft.

DIFFICULTIES: An easy and straightforward hill-ramble. No difficulties to speak of.

ACCOMMODATION: Hotels, guest-houses and bed-and-breakfast in Aberfoyle and Callander.

AN unwritten rule in hill-walking proclaims that it's not always the biggest hill which is best. Standing at a mere 1,520 ft above sea level, Ben A'an has much more character than many loftier giants of the north.

Drive north from Aberfoyle, in Stirlingshire, over the Duke's Road to The Trossachs, and stop for a moment at the top. The area which lies before you is wonderfully rugged and bristling with craggy hills and a plethora of mixed woodland and forest. Add to that mixture some lochs, and you have the magic mix that creates The Trossachs, the Highlands in miniature, some say.

Away in front of you a long line of hills approaches from the east, and at the western end of this chain, sticking up like a stumpy thumb, is the crest of Ben A'an, one of the finest viewpoints in the area and a short walk suitable for all but the most unfit.

Ben A'an isn't the hill's original name. That was Am Binnein, or the Rocky Peak, which well describes its craggy upper flanks, beloved of many Glasgow-based rock-climbers. The hill lies on the north shores of Loch Achray, close to the turreted grandeur of The Trossachs Hotel. At the foot of the path which runs up to the summit, the Forestry Commission has made a car-park and erected a signpost pointing the way.

At first, the hill climbs quite steeply through the woods, so take your time and enjoy it. Listen to the belling of tits and the song of the chaffinch, cheery sounds which will accompany every step. After a while, the steepness relents and a signpost indicates a viewpoint to the left. It's well worth taking time to have a look, for this viewpoint gives you a first glimpse of the rocky summit of the hill, nicely framed by spruce and larch.

FIRST PEAKS

I first came up this hill as a youngster, eager to stand on top of a mountain on my own. I'll never forget the thrill of seeing this top for the first time . . . it could have been my first sighting of Everest from Kala Pattar, in Nepal. From here the summit looks steep and exposed, but it deceives you. The path actually traverses behind the summit and carries you right on to the top without having to climb or scramble at all.

Once you leave the forest, the views open up towards the craggy bluffs and corries of Ben Venue and the long stretch of Loch Katrine,

Forestry Commission

Footpath to Ben An ›

THE FOOTPATH to Ben A'an. The path starts from a Forestry Commission car park at the foot of the hill, crosses the road and climbs up through the forest. Beyond the forest there is a steep rough section of path, but shouldn't present any real difficulties.

probably the areas most scenic loch. In late August and early September the heather blooms in purple magnificence and contrasts with the vibrancy of the emerald trees. Later the grasses turn blond, the leaves lighten and then seem to catch fire in a magnificent display of autumnal russet, red and gold. It's then that The Trossachs area is at its most beautiful.

MACGREGOR COUNTRY

The path climbs more steeply now, and is more broken underfoot. Take care on the wet ground. The path contours round the back of the hill, across some wet, mossy areas, and then up the last few feet to the summit. And what a fine rocky eyrie this is. The views towards the west are the best. On clear days the Arrochar hills are sharply defined, from the outline of The Cobbler, probably difficult to identify from this angle, to Ben Vorlich. Further north, the Crianlarich hills come into view, with the twin summits of Stobinian and Ben More particularly clear. Loch Katrine stretches out deep into Macgregor country, and across the waters below you lies the ancient pass of Bealach nam Bo, where, according to local legend, the Macgregors once drove their stolen cattle.

Take time to enjoy the summit, and if you're so inclined, try to sprint up the Ten Second Slab, the rocky boiler-plate slab which leans up to the actual summit. It's claimed that good climbers will scale it in 10 seconds. Ordinary pedestrians will take somewhat longer . . .

Ben Ledi, Loch Lomond and The Trossachs

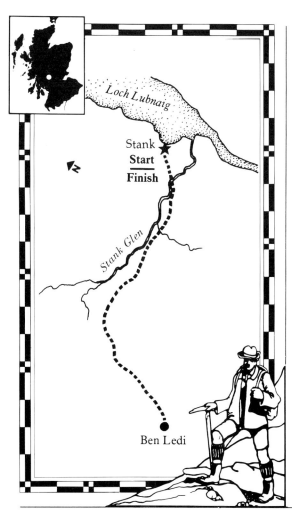

MAP: Ordnance Survey Sheet 57

DISTANCE: Six miles.

ASCENT: 2,500 ft.

DIFFICULTIES: An easy and straightforward hill-walk. The only potential, problem is getting lost in the forest, or drowning in the mud of the official Forestry Commission trail!

ACCOMMODATION : Hotels, guest-houses and bed-and-breakfast in Callander, Aberfoyle and Lochearnhead, Camp-site in Callander.

Ben Ledi is the mountain which dominates the western shore of Loch Lubnaig as you drive north from Callander towards Lochearnhead. Its ascent is supremely rewarding, for the view from the summit in clear conditions is quite outstanding.

On a long backpacking trip around the Trossachs a few years ago, I climbed Ben Ledi from Glen Finglas, an unusual angle of attack, but came across a summit view which was entirely unexpected. I quote from an earlier book, *Backpacker's Scotland*.

'Rather than follow a direct line up the steep slopes to the summit, I traversed a little northwards, and climbed the gentler north-west ridge by way of some pleasant grassy gullies. As I reached the summit ridge, the white trig point which indicates the summit stood out like a beacon against the dark-blue of the sky. The view was superb. All of the south, from the flats of

Flander's Moss to as far as the eye could see, was covered by an ocean of cloud, with only the high tops of the Campsie Fells piercing the whiteness. Ben Lomond, the Beacon Hill, stood out as its name suggests it should, and to the north of it, the unmistakable outline of The Cobbler dominated the higher of the Arrochar Alps. All the Crianlarich and Glen Falloch hills could be easily identified, rising to the twin spires of Stob Binnein and Ben More. To the north-east, Ben Vorlich was hidden by its close neighbour, Stuc a Chroin, and beyond them, the great Lawers massif stood out clearly, white-fringed with snow against the blue. Below me, Loch Lubnaig and the Pass of Leny were barely discernible through a gossamer-thin film of mist, but the village of Callander was still submerged in cloud.'

No-one seems to be able to give the exact derivation of the name Ledi. The original Gaelic gives it as Beinn Lididh, and an old *Statistical Account* suggests a possible derivation in the name Ben le Dia, the Hill of God. It seems this god could well have been the ancient sungod Baal, for the ancient Druids celebrated their annual Beltane, or May Day, rituals on the hill's summit.

To add to the weird goings-on, a small lochan lies about a mile north of the summit. This is known as Lochan nan Corp, or the Small Loch of the Corpses. Centuries ago a small cortege of mourners was following an old coffin road across the hill from Glen Finglas to St Bride's Chapel in the Pass of Leny. It was winter and as they crossed

THE VIEW from the summit of Ben Ledi looking to Loch Lubnaig. On the left is Ardnandave Hill, and just to the right of it, at the bend of the loch, the entrance to Glen Ample, Ben Ledi offers some of the best views in the Southern Highlands.

THE HILLS of the west, Loch Katrine from the summit of Ben A'an. The boy is scrambling up the summit boulder. It's claimed that the record for scrambling up this summit slab is 10 seconds. If you do it inside a minute you'll be doing quite well.

the frozen surface of the lochan, the ice cracked open and several of the mourners drowned in the freezing waters. A cheery place!

The Pass of Leny, just north of Callander, is a real gateway to the Highlands, pushing through from the rich and flat Lowlands into a jumble of hills that mark the beginnings of the Highlands. Drive through the pass for about half-a-mile before turning off left, over the Leny Water, to a car-park provided by the Forestry Commission. From here two roads head north towards Loch Lubnaig. Take the left-hand one.

Pass some cottages and continue on the road towards the farmhouse at Sark, and just before you reach it, take the forestry track which runs off to the left. At a sharp and obvious hairpin bend, a path leads off from the road up through the trees. This takes you up through the forest and into the Stank Glen. This place is thick with trees, as most modern plantations are, and there is often a heavy atmosphere. Indeed, it can be ominously gloomy, and you find yourself tramping on, up the dark tunnel to the light at the end, and the openness of the upper glen. And what a wild and hidden corner this is. On the hillside above lie a jumble of vast glacial erratics, boulders of immense size and strange shape. Many of them have an almost malignant look, broken clawing shapes 50 ft high, towering above pointing the way to Doom. They're weird, but fun if you enjoy a bit of scrambling.

Away to north the form of Arnandave Hill forms the sykline, and below is spread the forest like green velvet, with glimpses of Loch Lubnaig beyond. It's a grand place to be on a good, sunny day.

But the hill beckons, and it's not long up and on to the ridge, from where it's only a short hop to the summit. Follow the line of the old fenceposts which once marked the boundary between the estates.

2. Glen Coe

THE ROUNDING OF a certain bend to the left on the A92 Tyndrum to Fort William road across Rannoch Moor invariably stops conversation. It is preceeded by an air of expectancy, of anticipation, among a car's passengers. On the left a grassy bluff blocks the view. To the right the open moor pours onwards in flat desolation. Then, suddenly the view ahead is filled with a vision of a giant wedge-shaped mountain, growing stoutly from the flat mattress of the moor. Beyond it a row of mountains appears impenetrable, a wall of rock, riven and seamed by gullies and scree. The ribbon of road flows between them, a silver highway between rocky jaws. The contrast between the flatness of the Moor and the sudden verticalities of the crags is sudden and dramatic; and coming upon it is an experience which has impressed travellers for centuries.

Early writers commented on the scene, albeit with differing enthusiasms. Dorothy Wordsworth wrote: 'A huge peak, black and huge, as if with voluntary power instinct, upreared its head.' Charles Dickens was equally descriptive, if a little over-awed: 'Glen Coe itself is perfectly terrible . . . an awful place . . . scores of glens high up, which form such haunts as you might imagine yourself wandering in, in the very height and madness of a fever'. But a visitor to the nearby Kingshouse Inn in 1792 was unimpressed, and described the mountain, Buachaille Etive Mor, as 'a carcass of a mountain, peeled sore and hideously disgustful . . .'

Others were enraptured. Victorian painters exaggerated the verticalities and the vapours and longed to add some Alpine Valkyries; poets and writers allowed their fantasies to explode, and squeezed out actuality and fact for romance and rhapsody of Ossianic proportions. It was the start of the tourist boom, a boom, that was to change the persona of this place for evermore.

Glen Coe has been much maligned in the past 300 years. Its emotional, and somewhat twee, misnomer, Glen O' Weeping, has more place in a romantic Victorian novel than in reality.

OTHER MASSACRES

Yes, there was a massacre, made all the more dire because the sacred code of Highland hospitality was violated by Government troops, but other sacred codes of conduct were violated in those troubled days, too. Why has there been no long-lasting remembrance of the MacDonalds of Clanranald, who surrounded and set fire to the church at Trumpan while the MacLeods were worshipping within; or the MacDonells of Glen Garry who took a similar vengeance on the Mackenzies at the church of Urray in mid-Ross?

The MacLeods of Dunvegan wiped out the population of Eigg by suffocating them in a cave where they had hidden; and the hapless Neish clan were wiped out on their island home by the MacNabs as they lay recovering from a night of freebooter boozing – massacred with a hangover to boot!

But it's a sad day when you can still see a sign in a Glen Coe hostelry which reads: 'No Tinkers, No Vagrants and No Campbells'. One puts it down to tourism, the great God at whose shrine so many have to bow in obeisance. Many worse things are committed in its name.

WILD SCENERY

No, Glen Coe is deserving of far more than the tourist tear-jerking, although it's becoming harder and harder to escape the crass journalism of the tourist brochures. It's even been proclaimed that Glen Coe is known as the Glen O'Weeping because it rains all the time! It doesn't rain all the time in Glen Coe, and neither do the people of the glen go about sticking needles into Clan Campbell dolls.

The scenery of Glen Coe *is* uncompromisingly wild, and, like many other areas of Highland Scotland, it can be gloomy when the weather glowers. It can be stark, and it can be awesome. But it's always majestic, and it's bare-faced grandeur ranks it second-to-none in these islands of ours. Despite the fact that its 11-mile length is flanked by only three mountains on the south side and a long, notched ridge of mountain wall to the north, it gives the impression of being a deep trough cut through a veritable jumble of peaks and spires. But those mountains, Buachaille Etive Mor, 3,345 ft, Buachaille Etive Beag, 3,129 ft, and

THE REAL Ben Nevis. The stunning crags above the Allt a' Mhuillin, a climbers playground in winter and in summer. Some of the popular and classic routes include the North East Buttress, Tower Ridge and Observatory Ridge, routes which though long are not difficult for those with experience of some scrambling and basic rock climbing.

LOOKING BACK across the switchbacked ridges of the Mamores from the summit of Stob Ban. A traverse of the entire Mamore Ridge is an exhilerating walk but should be left until you are feeling fit.

THE GREEN Lochan, Lochan Uaine, where it's claimed the local faeries wash their clothes. From the slopes of Meall a Buachaille. An ascent of this hill is a worthwhile outing when the weather is too bad for the high Cairngorms.

LOCH AVON and th
outline of the squ
cut Shelterstone Crag
The Shelterstone itse
lies amid a great pile
bus sized boulders at
foot of the crag and is
capable of sleeping ha
dozen folk in some
comfort.

Bidean nam Bian, 3,766 ft, to the south, and the Aonach Eagach ridge to the north have between them some 26 tops which, with all their spurs and outliers, give the impression of being a complete and sizeable mountain range.

THE BUACHAILLE

The floor of the trough, the glen itself, is a green place, with fields and a loch, Loch Achtriochtan, and when the clouds lift and the sun smiles, it can be a place of immense, sparkling beauty, a place where the heartbeats quicken at the sight, where the sheer and absolute harmony of God's creation can stop you dead in your tracks, just as that first sighting of the Buchaille Etive Mor does at the very gates of Glen Coe.

This Great Shepherd of Etive, or, as it's popularly called, The Buachaille, stands in the angle between Glen Etive and Glen Coe, and simply dominates its surroundings. Its main ridge flanks Glen Etive for a good four miles, but it presents its finest aspect towards the Moor of Rannoch and the busy A82 road. The sharply-pointed peak is called Stob Dearg, the Red Peak, a name derived from the reddish rhyolite of the upper slopes. It rises above walls of sheer rock, splintered and riven by gullies and buttressed by a complex pattern of steep ridges and pillars.

To mountaineers everywhere, this is a special place, a spiritual home to thousands who, since the end of last century, have tackled the long ridges and deep, dark gullies, balanced on the delicate footholds of the steep walls, and from the summit enjoyed the prospect across the Rannoch Moor eastwards and northwards across the Mamores to Ben Nevis and beyond.

The very names of the mountain's features bring a quickening of the spirit to those who love such places: Crowberry Tower, the Rannoch Wall, and the Curved Ridge. Classic summer climbs – Agag's Groove and January Jigsaw – juggle in the memory with winter desperates such as Raven's Gully. During the short winter days, visiting climbers from all over the world try their hand at what is a unique form of mountaineering, Scottish mixed snow- and ice-climbing.

Traditionally, the whole valley, from Rannoch Moor, through the jaws between the Buachaille and the hills north of Altnafeith, and all the way to the sea at Loch Leven, is called Glen Coe. In fact, the headwaters of the Coe itself start beyond The Buachaille, high on the hillside beside the track known as the Devil's Staircase, which zig-zags its way up and over the hill to Kinlochleven.

This is an old military road, built by General Caulfeild in 1750 and now used by a new brand of infantrymen and women, the ramblers and backpackers following the route of the West Highland Way from Glasgow to Fort William. It's an easy walk of about four miles, but can be very different in winter, as many of Caulfeild's soldier navvies found to their cost. Later, at the beginning of this century, when the Blackwater dam was being built above Kinlochleven, a work-camp was set up for the mainly Highland and Irish navvies who worked on the project. Many of them died from exposure on the wild flanks of the Devil's Staircase as they walked to and from the Kingshouse Hotel, their bodies being discovered only in the spring when the snow melted. A superb book, *Children of the Dead End*, written by Irishman Patrick MacGill, tells the story graphically.

A mile or so west of the Devil's Staircase, a miniature Buachaille rears its head. This is Buachaille Etive Beag, the Little Shepherd of Etive, and its reflection can be beautifully cast on the still waters of Lochan na Fola, the Little Loch of Blood. This name commemorates an incident of 1543, when some men of Rannoch carried out a raid on the cattle belonging to Cunningham of Glenure.

By following the cattle dung, the Cunninghams realised that the beasts were to be taken across Rannoch Moor by way of Glen Coe, so they took a short cut and surprised the cattle thieves as they rested at the side of the lochan. The Rannoch men were struck down and their bodies thrown into the water. Another story claims that the lochan got its name after a quarrel over the division of a Christmas gift of cheese. Take your choice . . .

THE WEE BUACHAILLE

Stunning as the reflections of the wee Buachaille on the waters of Lochan na Fola may be, the real view of Glen Coe is from the true head of the glen, a spot represented on old maps as The Study. This word, or more accurately, Stiddie, is broad Scots for Anvil, and the Gaelic for the rocky knoll nearby is Inneain a' Cheathaich, or Anvil of the Mist. The spot is therefore misrepresented in its English name, which just shows how the corruption of the original Gaelic can change the meaning of the original word completely.

From the 'Anvil' rock which gives the spot its name, the view down the glen is world-famous. Immediately below you the waters of the Allt Lairig Eilde crash over a rocky gore into the Coe. It's a spot hemmed in by crags and where a piper often plays, in full Highland dress, of course.

LOOKING EAST along the crest of the Aonach Eagach ridge, with Buachaille Etive Mor in the distant right. Most walkers tend to traverse the Aonach Eagach from east to west. This offers the best views and is probably marginally easier.

B UACHAILLE ETIVE Mor, the Great Shepherd of Etive, in high summer. The walkers route to the summit takes an obvious corrie which cannot be seen from this angle, but scramblers and climbers are happy to ascend the hill by way of the Curved Ridge, which climbs the hill in the centre of its steep face.

After periods of heavy rain, the waterfall and the roar from the gorge are impressive. The river continues through a series of deep, green pools to another confluence called The Meeting of the Three Waters.

The views from The Study show clearly the definition of the Three Sisters of Glen Coe, the subject of MacCulloch's famous painting which hangs in the Art Gallery in Glasgow. These three spurs, Beinn Fhada, Gearr Aonach and Aonach Dlubh, are all outliers of Bidean nam Bian, the highest hill in the old county of Argyll. They project into the flatness of the glen in fine symmetry, huge rounded bulkheads of black, shining crag, the middle one, Gearr Aonach, showing a slimmer profile than her two matronly sisters.

Across the glen, the long, tortuous ridge of the Aonach Eagach is clearly seen, a jagged outline against the sky, Alpine-looking in winter raiment and offering a fine challenge to walkers and mountaineers.

Below the crags and the grey screes, the road winds, then straightens, past the waters of Loch Achtriochtan (where, it is claimed, water sprites once lived) and the strange, elongated slit in the cliff high above. This is Ossian's Cave, which can be reached only by a rock-climb of 200 ft or so.

Many fine combinations of hill walks wait to be enjoyed in the Glen Coe area, but some experience is necessary, as the mountains are steep-sided and fairly serious. Much of the area is owned by the National Trust for Scotland, bought in 1935, largely through the benevolence of one man, a great lover of the hills, Percy John Henry Unna.

It's said that Unna gave away a fortune to buy

THE GRACEFUL summit of Stob Coire nan Lochan, with the buttresses of Bidean nam Bian behind, and the walls of Aonach Dubh in the foreground, as seen from the Aonach Eagach ridge.

THE GREAT wall of the west face of Aonach Dubh from Glen Coe. There is an awesome character to Glen Coe created by the close proximity of the high peaks to the roadside. It's a feeling that can sometimes be overwhelming.

wilderness, but he was a man of foresight and great vision. Aware of potential problems of access and wild land 'development', he formulated the 'Unna Rules'. With clear and fixed ideas of land-management, he wrote to the council of the NTS with equally clear conditions for his involvement in the purchase. The Trust was asked to ensure that the land be maintained in its 'primitive' condition for all time, with unrestricted access for the public. Sheep-farming and cattle-grazing could continue, but stalking, other than the annual cull, must cease. He wanted no man-made structures. The mountains should not be made safer and easier to climb. Paths should not be extended or improved, nor new paths made; and he objected to signposts, paint-marks, and marker cairns other than those showing that the land was owned by the National Trust for Scotland.

ERODED PATHS

It's sad that the NTS has chosen to ignore those Unna Rules, treating them largely today as mere guidelines. Footpaths wriggle their eroded way into the high glens. Signposts point out the routes. Car-parks have been built, and bridges put over the rivers to give access to the hills. And a new visitor centre has been built at Clachaig. An ongoing battle against erosion costs the Trust thousands of pounds every year. Percy Unna's worst fears have been realised in a most unfortun-ate way.

Beyond the Visitor Centre a path leads through the woods to a high knoll, popularly known as the Signal Rock. This is *not* where Campbell of Glenlyon gave the signal to start the Massacre of February 13, 1692, but the rock from which the MacDonald chiefs used to summon

their clan in times of emergency.

Beyond Clachaig, the old road to Carnoch village, commonly known as Glencoe Village, winds through the woods, but the new road carries on past the Visitor Centre and past the old village of Achnacon, which was destroyed during the Massacre of 1692, burned to the ground on the cold February night. Beyond this the character of the glen changes from being wild, narrow and mountainous, to broad, pastoral and gentle. A brooding stillness often hangs over the village, especially in winter, when the smoke from the chimneys drifts straight up into the air and the older whitewashed houses seem to huddle together for warmth. Here in Carnoch, near the old Bridge of Coe stands a unique Celtic cross which states simply:

In memory of MacIan, Chief of Glencoe, who fell with his people in the Massacre of Glencoe.

MacIan is buried on Eilean Munde on Loch Leven, the ancient burial isle of the Macdonalds of Glencoe. His death, and the unfortunate events which have been recorded in history as the Massacre of Glencoe, staggered public opinion for decades, not for the brutality of the slaughter, but because it was planned by men in high public positions, and because they used the victims' traditional hospitality as a means of murdering them, and because the king of the time, William of Orange, approved the plans.

Out of an adult population of about 150, 40 were killed. It seems that many of the soldiers involved hadn't the stomach to carry out the orders of their southern masters. Many other MacDonalds fled half-naked to the snowy mountains in an attempt to escape, but

succumbed to the freezing conditions of Glen Coe's winter hills.

But public concern soon caused the Parliament of the day to condemn the Massacre as 'Murder Under Trust', and a commission of inquiry was set up. At the end of the day no-one was punished, and although the Campbells who were behind the infamy escaped real legal justice, their name was for many years firmly associated with treachery.

Glen Coe has today shrugged off its mantle of tragedy, at least where the Tourist Board has allowed, and it is a place popular with walkers and climbers, campers and those who like simply to drive through and gape at the raw and natural beauty of it. It's a priceless asset to the nation, a rich jewel in the crown of Scotland's scenic grandeur, a place worth protecting for future generations.

Buachaille Etive Mor

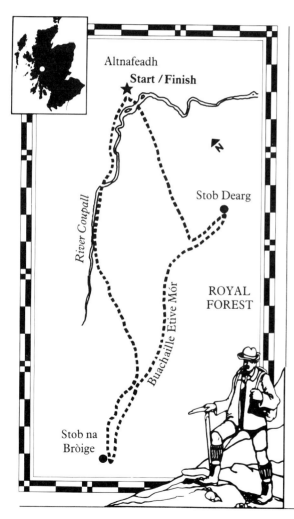

Altnafeadh
Start / Finish

River Coupall

Stob Dearg

Buachaille Etive Mór

ROYAL
FOREST

Stob na
Bròige

MAP: Ordnance Survey Sheet 41.

DISTANCE: Four miles.

ASCENT: 2,500 ft.

DIFFICULTIES: A straightforward mountain walk, but take care in spring and early summer, when cornices overhang the lip of Coire na Tulaich. Steep snow can also pose hazards on the upper slopes of this corrie, and ice-axes may be necessary well into the spring. The Curved Ridge route is suitable only for those with rock-climbing experience.

ACCOMMODATION: Youth hostel at Glen Coe. Private bunkhouses at Bridge of Orchy, Kingshouse and Glen Coe. Hotels, guest-houses and bed-and-breakfast at Bridge of Orchy, Kingshouse and Glen Coe. Camp-sites at Kingshouse and Glen Coe.

If ever a poll were taken to find the most popular mountain in Scotland, Buachaille Etive Mor, or the Great Herdsman of Glen Etive, would always rank in the Top Five.

Rising majestically from the western edge of Rannoch Moor, it forms an impressive cornerstone between Glen Coe and Glen Etive. Its pyramid shape, thrown up from its squat, solid base, is without doubt the epitome of classical mountain lines. What's more, those very lines, steep and uncompromising, throw down a gauntlet to every passer-by. The great walls, ridges and gullies present an air of impregnability, offering few lines of access. For that very reason, many walkers prefer to pass on to look for easier pickings.

But one magnificent route does sneak an easier way to the top of this steep and imposing face. It's a route for those who don't mind using their hands now and again, and who won't be intimated by steep drops and lots of exposure. The Curved Ridge, as it is known, is in fact a climber's descent route and is graded officially as a 'moderate' rock-climb. I tell you that because it is a climb rather than a walk, and although it really falls outside the scope of this book, it is too good to miss completely.

The route, as its name suggests, curves its way up from near the base of the mountain, following the crest of a broad solid, ridge. Much of the route involves steep scrambling, but the holds are generally big and generous. As you climb higher, so the steepness relents, and the route to the summit goes via the base of the impressive Crowberry Tower and up some easily-scrambled rocks to the 3,345 ft Stob Dearg top of Buachaille Etive Mor.

FOUR TOPS

This top is in fact one of four tops. The Buachaille is really a four-mile-long ridge which rises steeply above Glen Etive with its four tops well spaced along its length.

But The Buachaille isn't only a climber's and scrambler's mountain. The walker's breach in the mountain's defences is Coire na Tulaich, directly behind the whitewashed climbing hut of

THE CLASSIC view of the Buachaille Etive Mor from Blackrock Cottage. The mountain, the Great Herdsman of Glen Etive is world famous for its range of rock and snow and ice climbs. Mountaineers come from all corners of the earth to test themselves on its steep crags.

Lagangarbh, at the north-west side of the hill. A track crosses the River Coupall by a footbridge and makes its way up into the corrie beyond the hut.

In no time you are in a real mountain atmosphere as the path subtly climbs rocky slopes and terraces before taking up the steepness above in a series of zig-zags. Beetling crags rise above you, and the view behind is framed by a truncated 'V' formed by the outer slopes of the corrie. Beyond lie the Blackwater Reservoir, Loch Trieg and the Loch Ossian hills.

Take care on the last few hundred feet, especially if climbers are below you. The scree hereabouts is loose and friable, and easily kicked down on those below you. Care is needed and you would do well to avoid the obvious narrowing gully at the top of the slope. Scramble up the steep ground east of the gully to top-out on the broad ridge above. Ahead lies the great jumble of peaks that make up the Blackmount Deer Forest. To your left are the remaining slopes which lead you to the top of Stob Dearg while to your right the impressive wedge of Stob na Doire rises from the ridge *bealach*.

PEAT AND BOG

The ridge leading to the summit of Stob Dearg is strewn with loose rock and is fairly rough going, but a path of sorts winds through the biggest of the boulders. As you approach the summit, the ridge narrows nicely, and after one or two false summits you will reach the large cairn which appears to sit on the very edge of nothing.

This feeling is exaggerated because of the flatness and the vastness of Rannoch Moor, which lies below you. On its outer edges, the Bridge of Orchy hills, the Perthshire hills, the Ben Alder group, and the Blackwater hills form the rough bounds, effectively containing this great mattress of peat and bog. Behind you the rest of the Glen Coe peaks lift their heads proudly, culminating in Bidean nam Bian, the highest hill in the old county of Argyll. Through the tight jaws of Glen Coe, the newish Ballachulish Bridge is well framed, joining the two shores of Loch Leven.

The descent is the same as the way up, but the energetic may like to add the other tops of the mountain, Stob na Doire, Stob Coire Altruim and Stob na Broige. The return to Lagangarbh is best made by returning over Stob Coire Altruim to the bealach at grid reference 203531, just before Stob na Doire. From there you can easily descend north-north-west into the Lairig Gartain and the path which returns to the A82 just west of Lagangarbh.

Aonach Eagach Ridge

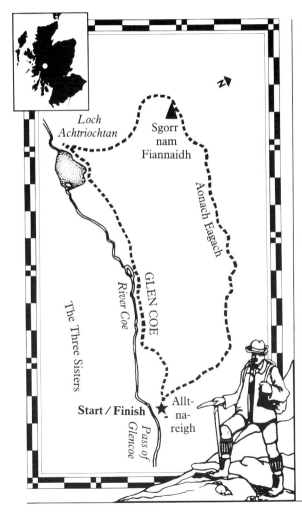

MAP: Ordnance Survey 41.

DISTANCE: Six miles.

ASCENT: 3,200 ft.

DIFFICULTIES: This walk is for experienced mountain-walkers with some scrambling experience. If you don't have that experience, go with an experienced companion and take a rope. In winter the route is a serious snow- and-ice climb, a mountaineering expedition. You are not recommended to leave the ridge after Am Bodach until you have reached Sgor nam Fiannaidh.

ACCOMMODATION: Youth hostel, bunk-house and camp-sites in Glencoe. Hotels, guest-houses and bed-and-breakfast in Glencoe, Ballachulish and Onich.

Try saying Oen-ach Ay-ach if you're having difficulty. It means Notched Ridge, and that well describes it. This is the huge, broken and gully-riven wall that forms the northern barrier of Glen Coe. The ridge is more than two miles long and offers two Munros, Meall Dearg, 3,119 ft, and Sgorr nam Fiannaidh, 3,173 ft, and lots of heart-stopping moments if you're not used to a modicum of exposure.

As with the Innaccessible Pinnacle in Skye, the mere mention of the Aonach Eagach occasionally makes walkers flinch, but, like the Inn-Pin, it shouldn't be missed. Here is an experience worth all the nervous tension you can muster. As they say in Ireland, it's a broth of a walk – more of a scramble, actually, with some

pretty meaty stuff.

The hard fact of the matter is that the route is officially classed as a Grade 1 rock-climb, but don't panic. That doesn't necessarily mean that it is hard. All it means is that here and there you're going to need your hands, and at one or two points you'll have to look up instead of looking down – unless you've a good head for heights, of course. In winter it's classed as a Grade 3 winter climb, which is a different ball-game altogether and puts it completely into the realm of ropework, belays, ice-axes and crampons. So what we're talking about here is a summer job, preferably in dry, clear conditions.

One encouraging point is that navigation isn't usually a problem. Once you've started on the ridge, you're advised to stick with it to the end, and you don't have much option. Both sides are steep and loose, and don't encourage wandering. But the ridge itself, for most of it's length, is easy and obvious. The scrambling sections are more exhilarating than serious, and the whole route is reckoned to be the finest ridge on the mainland. It certainly doesn't expose you to the type of problem you'll find on the Cuillin Ridge on Skye, and technically it's easier than the Rhum Cuillin and probably more akin to the Isle of Arran ridges.

On my first visit to the Aonach Eagach I was still impressed by the myths that surround this ridge, so much so that my mate and I took a rope with us. There we were, on the first steep section,

ON THE Aonach Eagach ridge, looking west from Meall Dearg. It is suggested that you shouldn't leave the ridge until you reach the other end. Travelling westwards has the advantage of being able to drop down off the hill and straight into the bar of the Clachaig Inn.

busy roping up, when a party of Girl Guides overtook us, skipping gaily up the steep rock without a hint of protection. Red-faced, we stuffed the rope into our pack and followed on at a suitable distance.

Start at the car-park just west of Allt-na-reigh on the A82 road, and follow the signposted path which climbs steeply north-east from the roadside. Higher up the hillside are two alternative routes. The better one stays with the original path over the crest of the south-east ridge into a narrow corrie on the east side of Am Bodach. A burn runs down from the top and you follow this to reach the main ridge at the saddle north-east of the Am Bodach summit. From here, easy slopes lead to the summit and your first views of the ridge stretching ahead.

POLISHED ROCK

It's a fairly daunting sight, this switchbacked fin of rock and grass, steep-sided and exposed, with occasional pinnacles posing as obstacles at points along its length. But enjoy the prospect, away to the north, of the Mamores and Ben Nevis and the hills beyond, and on the other side, the peaks and ridges of the Bidean nam Bian massif, thrown up from the deep depths of Glen Coe. This is the point of no return . . .

The first difficult stretch is encountered straight away. You've no time to ease yourself into it, I'm afraid. A sudden drop appears, with about 50 ft of scrambling on fairly polished rock. But don't let is phase you. Face in and look for the holds. They're there, all right. Just take your time and look for them, and soon you'll be traversing on good holds on to the crest of the ridge, where an easy gradient takes you on to a top beyond which lie the final slopes to the first Munro top, Meall Dearg, The Red Hill.

The next section is the best. Here like the Crazy Pinnacles, the rocky teeth which give the ridge its name. Follow the obvious path and the scratch-marks on the rock and enjoy the sections of pretty-easy scrambling on good rock. Some of the scrambling can be avoided by flanking the pinnacles, while many walkers actually enjoy the security of the big holds above what is often huge exposure.

The final two pinnacles offer most scrambling, before a dip in the ridge immediately before Sob Coire Leith indicates the end of the difficulties. This is where you get a chance to breathe deeply and relax, and wander at ease over the remainder of the ridge, broad and user-friendly, to the last summit and the second Murno, Sgor nam Fiannaidh, The Rocky Peak of the Fingalians.

Continue westwards along the ridge, enjoying the remarkable views down the length of Loch Leven to Ardgour. Then descend south-eastwards into a small corrie, from where steep, rocky slopes lead you down to the roadside near Loch Achtriochtan. Many walkers are tempted into a descent which will lead them directly to the Clachaig Inn and a foaming pint, but you're likely to find yourself on steep and difficult ground, with prospects of a pint of beer fading at the same rate as the daylight. Likewise, the path that runs up the hill, just west of the obvious cleft of the Clachaig Gully, is not really suitable for descent either. You're likely to knock loose rock into the gully, where rock-climbers could well be at grips with the water-worn rock. It's not the best way to make yourself popular.

LOOKING TOWARDS the Crazy Pinnacles section of the Aonach Eagach ridge. This section is the most interesting part of the entire ridge. There are only one or two points where there are real difficulties, and it is generally thought that the hardest move is up a chimney on one of the pinnacles.

Bidean Nam Bian

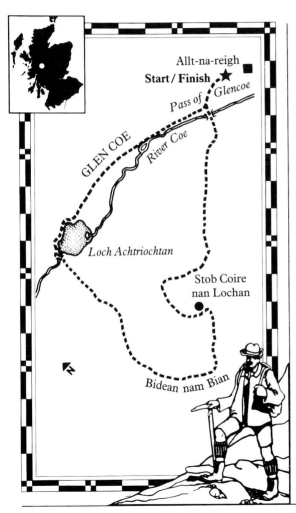

MAP: Ordnance Survey Sheet 41.

DISTANCE: Six miles.

ASCENT: 4,000 ft.

DIFFICULTIES: This is serious mountain country and demands care and experience. However, the ridges and corries tend to be well frequented, especially in holiday periods. Navigational skills are essential, and so is the ability to use an ice-axe in spring and early summer, and often even in late autumn into winter. The ridges can be Alpine in winter, and then demand skill in ice-axe and crampon techniques.

ACCOMMODATION: Youth hostel in Glencoe. Bunk-houses at Kingshouse and Glen Coe. Hotels, guest-houses and bed-and-breakfast in Glen Coe, Kingshouse and Ballachulish.

In a rather satisfying way, Bidean nam Bian, the highest hill in the old county of Argyll, is very much a mountaineer's mountain. Like so many of the Cairngorms' tops, it's difficult to identify this hill from the roadside as you can, say, the Buachaille. Bidean retires shyly behind its outliers, great hills in themselves, and reserves its own splendours for those who take the trouble to climb its steep flanks and ridges. This is a hill that extracts its quart of sweat and toil from the visitor.

Bidean nam Bian, or Peak of the Mountains, is well named, for this summit is thrown up by four great ridges which give way to nine separate summits and cradle three deep and distinctive corries, well worth visiting in their own right. It rises 3,772 ft above the level of Loch Leven, and

you have to earn every one of them; but no matter which route you choose, you have splendid mountain grandeur around you from the start.

SUMMER OUTING

For the purposes of this book, Bidean is a summer outing. In winter the ridges spout great snow cornices, overhanging the deep-cut corries, many of them prone to avalanche. This is a mountaineer's mountain in more ways than one. Years ago I took some friends up Bidean in early November. There didn't seem to be a lot of snow about, but higher up, above the 3,000 ft contour, we found enough to make things tricky. We had two ice-axes between seven of us! With one brave soul out in front, hacking steps in the iron-hard snow, we followed him to the summit, but while my inexperienced friends delighted in the success of achieving the summit, I was worried sick about how we would get back down.

I vaguely hoped that we could descend into the Coire Ghabhail, from which we could return to the Glen Coe road, but, as I had half-expected, its steep and precipitous slopes were also swathed in hard snow, so, leaving one of the more experienced of the party to descend into the Coire Ghabhail, using the two ice-axes, from where he would go down to the road to fetch a car, we descended south-east into Glen Etive, leaving us with a long and tiring walk out. We all learned a lesson that day.

A number of alternative routes ascend Bidean

S TOB COIRE NAN
 Lochan from the
slopes of Bidean nam
Bian. This top and Stob
Coire nam Beith are
outliers of Bidean which
is more like a small range
of mountains rather than
a single mountain.

nam Bian, but one or two have been over-promoted and have suffered gross erosion. The route I recommend is a fine circular route, with a short distance of road-walking at the end.

Leave the A82 road opposite Coire nan Lochan, cross the bridge over the River Coe, and take the track that climbs up into the corrie below the great East Face of Aonach Dubh. The path runs all the way to the head of the corrie, where three lochans reflect the steep crags above which led to the summit of Stob Coire nan Lochan, one of Bidean's outliers.

From the lochans, climb the rocky slopes in a north-west direction to the high saddle between Aonach Mor and the long ridge which runs south and then east to Stob Coire nan Lochan.

Take the south-west ridge from the summit, and soon you'll be climbing quite steeply again, passing, in blissful ignorance, above the sheer crags of the Diamond and Churchdoor Buttresses. The summit of Bidean is, in fact, the junction of three narrow and airy ridges, an archtypal mountain-top which is impressive in clear conditions and almost Alpine in winter raiment.

The westward descent takes you down over Stob Coire nam Beith, the Peak of the Corrie of the Birch, and then down a well-worn path in Coire nam Beith to the shores of Loch Achtriochtan, below the beetling cliffs of Aonach Dubh and the unusual 'key-hole' slit of Ossian's Cave. A couple of miles on the road takes you back to the car.

Beinn Bheithir

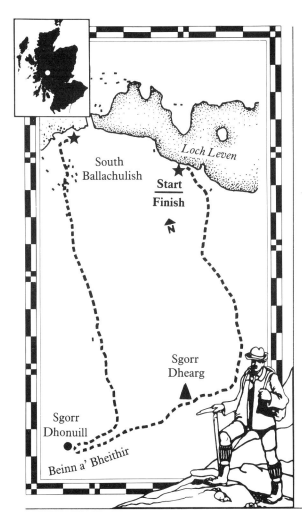

MAP: Ordnance Survey Sheet 41.

DISTANCE: Eight miles.

ASCENT: 4,200 ft.

DIFFICULTIES: A straightforward scramble and mountain-walk with no real difficulties other than navigating through perverse forestry. You may be lucky, and find a clear-felled area by the time you get there.

ACCOMMODATION: Youth hostel at Glen Coe. Hotels, guest-houses and bed-and-breakfast at Ballachulish, Onich, Glencoe and Fort William. Camp-sites in Glen Coe.

This hill, the Hill of the Thunderbolt, rises gracefully above the narrows of Loch Leven at Ballachulish. It is a fine mountain, made up of two peaks on a long, curving ridge, forming north-facing corries.

A major problem in reaching it, however, is to penetrate an almost impassible wall of conifers. It isn't easy, and I hope you have better luck in negotiating the trees than I've had in the past.

Leave the A828 road about half-a-mile west of Ballachulish Bridge and follow that minor road south-south-east for a few hundred yards to where a small group of houses huddles at the foot of Gleann a'Chaolais. You can leave your car here.

Follow the forestry road, walking due south, until after a little more than a mile it begins to zig-zag up some steeper ground. Just past an old quarry, you'll reach a crossroads. Cross over until you reach a concrete bridge over a burn. Just east of this burn, you'll find a cairn which marks the start of the path through the trees. This is where the fun starts.

Forestry planting has gone on here on a grand scale for years, giving the mountain a dark-green skirt which protects it from the mass feet of walkers and climbers. I thought I was clever, and could remember a thin, winding track through the trees I had taken umpteen years ago. I told my companion so, and assured him the plantation was no barrier. We would be on the rocky slopes within half-an-hour. It wasn't to be.

An hour later we were still struggling through a mass and jumble of clear-felled timber, an obstacle which tried its best to trip us up at every step. Annoyingly, the debris covered the route of the path, which we lost very quickly anyway.

However, we weren't going to allow that to spoil the day. Eventually, even though scratched and sweaty, we found the path and followed it steeply up through the forest, out of the dark conifers and into a high-level birch-wood. We could see the ridge above us, vanishing into the cloud. It still looked remote and unfriendly.

SORE LEGS

But the high-level corrie in which we found ourselves had real rocky character. A raven barked at us from a distance and deer coughed high up on the crag. We rambled our way up the hillside, testing ourselves on some of the craggy sections, playing at being mountaineers when we could more easily have tramped up the heather. But this scrambling takes your mind off sore legs. It transfers the thought processes to the problems immediately at hand – indeed, to where the next hand will go, testing the rock to see if it will hold, searching for the next foothold, checking to see that you're not getting into ground that's too difficult. It's a lot more fun than plodding.

But soon we reached the ridge, with the cloud playing hide-and-seek with us, in turn opening up vast panoramas over Loch Leven and Loch Linnhe to the hills of Ardgour, and then blanketing us in greyness, stifling, cold and damp. To our right was the peak, Sgorr Dhonuill, and we dutifully climbed the ridge to its summit before turning back on ourselves. The ridge wound on and snow was on the ground, emphasising the narrowness of the place. A trig pillar seemed out of character as it marked the summit of the other top of Beinn Bheithir, Sgorr Dhearg, the Red Peak. Next on the ridge was the Fair Peak, Sgorr Bhan, which seemed more appropriate as the weather improved, offering good views up and into the narrow clench of Glen Coe. You don't realise how narrow Glen Coe is until you see it from this angle.

By now the weather was improving rapidly, but, unfortunately, the daylight hours, few enough at this time of year, were dwindling remorselessly. These factors combined to create a marvellous diffused light, a pinkish-orange glow which softened the wild surroundings. It was a joy to descend the good path, high above the waters of Loch Leven and the old burial isle of the Glen Coe Macdonalds, Eilean Munde.

But the joy was short-lived. We still had to negotiate the forest and its own peculiar obstacle course. But by this time we had the added hazard that it was getting dark. We could barely see anything in the black tunnels through the plantations. We tripped and stumbled and cursed, and then we lost the line of the path. By the time we realised where we were, we could see the lights of Ballachulish way below us. We were too far east, so we had to back-track to follow the rocky line of a stream through the remaining plantations.

Eventually, we found a forestry road which took us down to the roadside, and were thankful for it. It's not often that the real obstacles of a hill-walk are found just a few minutes from the road, rather than on the wild, windswept ridges 3,000 ft up.

The Hospital Lochan

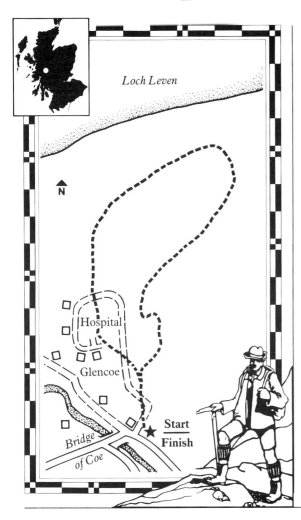

MAP: ordnance Survey Sheet 41.

DISTANCE: Two miles.

ASCENT: Negligible.

DIFFICULTIES: Nil.

ACCOMMODATION: Youth hostel in Glencoe. Hotels, guest-houses and bed-and-breakfast in Glencoe village. Camp-sites in Glen Coe.

While Glen Coe offers many magnificent hill- and mountain-walks, few of them are low-level, simply because the mountains fall sheer into the glen. But just north of Carnoch village, a large area of woodland at the foot of the Pap of Glencoe boasts some fine shorter walks, all in complete contrast to the serious nature of the mountains.

Take the road east through Carnoch village and cross the bridge over the River Coe. Shortly after the bridge, turn off to the left on the road towards Glencoe Hospital. Follow this road to the first turn-off, on the right, and continue along this road to the car-park.

The Forestry Commission has created three walks in this area, but none of them is arduous or serious, and if you have the time, about 90 minutes, the combination of the three makes a worthwhile outing.

Go through the larger of two gates and follow the path to the lochan, and then round the lochan in an anti-clockwise direction. Enjoy the rhododendron bushes, symbolic in many ways of the west Highlands, and the mixed woodland of pine, birch and rowan. Look out for the chaffinches, and the blue tits, coal tits and great tits. Often you'll see buzzards soaring in the thermals above, and, more often than not, ubiquitous black-head gulls floating on the waters of the lochan.

This lochan, which sits so naturally among the trees, with its fine backdrop of scree-girt mountains, is man-made. It was created in the mid-nineteenth century by Lord Strathcona, who lived in Glencoe House, the building that is now the hospital. His wife was apparently half Red Indian, and in an effort to appease her homesickness, he created this lochan in the woods. Sadly, his efforts were in vain. She continued to grieve for Canada, and the couple eventually returned to live there.

WALKING ROUND

At the far end of the lochan another path leads off to the left. This begins to climb quite steeply, and soon offers some fine views of the surrounding mountains, from the Pap of Glencoe to Bidian nam Bian and down Loch Leven to the Ballachulish hills.

Soon the track begins to descend back to the car-park, but instead of finishing, carry on to the left to the Peninsula Walk, a lovely circuit with some fine views towards Loch Leven and its island and down the loch towards Ballachulish Bridge.

The circuit bring you back naturally to the car-park, past a small lily-covered pond and the natural arch formed by two small trees. The entire circuit takes about 90 minutes and is a little more than two miles long.

Pap of Glen Coe

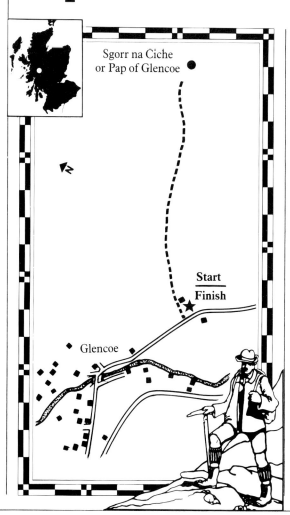

MAP: Ordnance Survey Sheet 41.

DISTANCE: Three miles there and back.

ASCENT: 2,300 ft.

DIFFICULTIES: Short, but steep.

ACCOMMODATION: Youth hostel in Glen Coe. Hotels, guest-houses and bed-and-breakfast in Glencoe village and Carnoch, and at Ballachulish and Onich. Camp-sites in Glen Coe.

Significantly smaller than most of the Glen Coe peaks, the Pap of Glencoe, or, to give it its proper name, Sgor na Ciche, offers comparatively finer views. This is often the case with smaller hills, as so often they give you the opportunity to have an eagle's-eye view of the bigger summits, rather than gaze at their foreshortened image from the roadside.

But the Pap of Glen Coe has other attributes. Positioned at the end of a long, tight ridge, it looks down steeply on one side to the waters of Loch Leven, snaking its way deeply inland to Kinlochleven, and on the other side to the deep and narrow cleft of Glen Coe itself.

In front of you Loch Leven narrows at Ballachullish Bridge, and then, beyond, Loch Linnhe opens out to front the mountain splendour of Argour, with craggy Garbh Beinn lording it over all. Because of all this spaciousness, the feeling of height is exaggerated.

THE SUMMIT of the Pap of Glen Coe. Although lower in height than most of the surrounding peaks, the summit of the Pap offers superb views not only in Glen Coe but down towards the hills of Ardgour, and back towards the Mamores.

LOOKING ACROSS to the Mamores and the rounded summit of Ben Nevis from the beginning of the Aonach Eagach ridge. Not only does this ridge offer a magnificient high level traverse, but the views both to the north and to the south are first class.

The summit, too, is a tight place, further adding to the feeling of exposure.

Unfortunatley, despite a lack of height, the Pap extracts a fair amount of energy in its ascent. Although the climb is straightfoward, it is steep, and I know of several individuals who have set off thinking it would be a doddle and that they could scramble up in half-an-hour. Not so!

GIANT LEGENDS

A fairly good path leads up the hill, starting about half-a-mile east of the Bridge of Coe on the old Glen Coe road. Climb the steep slopes and make for the obvious *bealach* between the Pap and its neighbouring peak. Sgor nam Fiannaidh, the Peak of the Fingalians.

The area has a number of Fingalian associations, including Ossian's Cave, which looks down on Loch Achtriochtan. Ossian was the bardic warrior son of Fingal, or, as he's known in Ireland, Fionn McCuhaill. These 'Fair-haired Giants' have a wealth of Celtic sagas woven around their exploits, and it's said that they roamed both Erin and Alba, setting up forts and warring with the locals. Name associations can be found all over the Highlands, including the Cairngorms, with the Corrie of the Battle of the Fingalians, near Beinn Bhrotain, and Ath na Fionn, on the River Avon.

Look carefully as you approach the summit and you'll see, on the west side, parallel smooth slabs of quartzite, ground out by glaciation, and, further down the slope, the remains of a series of trenches dug, it is believed, by Fingalian warriors as a defence against Norse invaders, the forces of the King of Lochlann as celebrated in the epic *Poems of Ossian*.

The final slopes to the summit are rocky, with a lot of loose stone, but the grandeur of the setting hits you forcibly once you reach the top.

To the north, the Mamores are set out in a long chain, with the rounded pate of Ben Nevis peeping over the top. Westwards, the blue hills of Ardgour tug the heart with that intangible pull of the west, while, closer at hand, the high-level ridge of Beinn Bheithir rises high above its skirts of conifer forest.

3. Lochaber

BEN NEVIS, BRITAIN'S highest mountain at 4,406 ft above sea level, has been described as a harlot, a 'mountain of loveless loveliness'. Brooding over the district of Lochaber, it appears as a round-shouldered bulk of a hill, often gaunt and dark, a mountain of many faces, of diverse character.

To some Ben Nevis presents the challenge of reaching and standing on the highest summit in the country, met by a long walk up a wide, rough track to a summit littered with man's feeble graffiti; the peeling ruins of an old weather observatory, an ugly corrugated-iron shelter, memorials to the victims of Hiroshima and old Fred, who climbed the Ben 50 times and eventually died in his bed in Barnsley. Didn't someone suggest this was Britain's highest midden?

GREAT CLIMBS

For thousands of people every year, to reach the top of Ben Nevis is their once-in-a-lifetime mountain experience, but for thousands more the Ben represents something infinitely finer. The brooding, round-shouldered aspect of the hill is a façade, a screen, protecting the real guts of the mountain. In reality, this is one of the great climbing mountains of the world. The north-east-facing two-miles stretch of cliffs which dominates the high corrie of the Allt-a Mhuillin presents an aspect of the hill which is both grand and stunning. This, the most formidable rock-face in Britain, is the dominant, if largely hidden, feature of Ben Nevis.

TERRIBLE BEAUTY

The high cliffs are riven and seared by gullies, prominent ridges, towers and buttresses. Generations of rock-climbers have pioneered long and difficult routes on the greasy rock, and when the mountain changes its face, chameleon-like, with the advent of winter snows, the climbers return to enjoy a type of mountaineering which is probably unique in the world – mixed winter climbing a pot-pourri of rock-scrambling and *sprachling*, balancing on small, snow-filled footholds, while hanging on to ice-axes with their tips tentatively embedded into layers of thin and brittle water-ice. All this while the wind throws down showers of fine, powdery spindrift from above, and the cold throbs through your body like toothache.

It's a masochistic experience, but the rewards are immense, if difficult to explain to those who don't understand. The great Louis Armstrong was once asked what it was, exactly, that he got out of playing the trumpet, Satchmo replied: 'Man, if you gotta ask that question, then you'll never know!' Scottish winter climbing is a bit like that, too.

The origin of the name Nevis is somewhat obscure, but the general belief is that it means 'terrible', from the old Irish Gaelic word *neamhaise*, or the Highland Gaelic word *ni-mhaise*, meaning 'no beauty'. Another school of thought believes the word comes from *Nimheis*, which could be 'heaven'. That old Highland *sennachie*, Seton Gordon, suggests that the name of the mountain has been taken from the river of the same name. Glen Nevis and its river apparently had a bad reputation in the old days. A sixteenth-century bard coined this verse:

Glen Nevis, a glen of stones,
A glen where corn ripens late,
A long, wild, waste glen,
With thievish folk of evil habit

How our perceptions have changed. Drive the length of Glen Nevis on any good day of high summer nowadays, and it will be full of people enjoying the atmosphere and the grandeur of it. The mountains and glens that once overawed people are now looked on with reverence and appreciation. Perhaps the dark, satanic mills and smog-filled towns and cities of the Industrial Revolution put such perceptions into a true perspective.

Fort William, which sprawls at the foot of Ben Nevis, shares the mountain's portrait of 'loveless loveliness'. The principal town of the West Highlands, Fort William is a busy and, in summer, crowded tourist centre. It has been said that the town is more functional than attractive, but for all that it has a buzz about it, created by that very function. It is a commercial centre for a

S TOB CHOIRE an
Laoigh in the Grey
Corries. The Grey
Corries get their name
from the amount of
quartzite which covers
the summit slopes. From
the north, on the road
between Roy Bridge and
Spean Bridge, this
quartz looks like snow.

THE TOURIST path which runs from Achintee in Glen Nevis to Ben Nevis. In the background lies Glen Nevis itself and Sgurr a Mhaim and Stob Ban. Sgurr a Mhaim is often mistaken for Ben Nevis because tourists generally mistake its quartz capped peak as being snow covered.

large radius of population, and as such has more apparent industry that most other Highland towns.

The pulp mill at the head of Loch Linnhe has a big influence in the town, and that, along with some haphazardly-planned housing schemes, new hotels, factories and a tangle of hydro-electric pylons, detract from the fine natural position of the place. It's an area of high unemployment, the largest employer being the British Alcan Company, whose damming activities and pipelines can be seen around much of the Lochaber area.

NEW DEVELOPMENT

Until now, Fort William has been a seasonal resort, but with the opening of the new Aonach Mor ski area, it's hoped that the town will begin to enjoy the same all-year-round prosperity which the Cairngorm ski area has brought to Strathsprey and Badenoch.

Aonach Mor is north-east of Ben Nevis, and the upper reaches of the mountain, particularly the long Snowgoose Gully, holds snow until well into early summer. Since getting the go-ahead for the development, the Fort William-based Nevis Ranges Development Company has wasted little time in starting what is probably the largest-ever environmental job to be undertaken in the UK. No tracked vehicle has been used on the hill, and all the transportation of men and materials has been by helicopters. Almost £1 million pounds' worth of flying time has been involved in the project. The new development will ensure a large number of new jobs to the Lochaber area, and guarantees a steady influx of visitors during winter, allowing many hotels and guest-houses to

stay open virtually all-year-round.

But for many other outdoors enthusiasts, especially climbers, For William has always been an all-year-round Mecca, a gateway to such mountains as the Ben, the Mamores, the Grey Corries, and a stopping-off point en route to the delights of the far north and west. The fort from which the town takes its name was destroyed in 1890 to make way for the West Highland Railway. First built by General Monk in 1655, it was later restructured during the reign of William III with the purpose of holding a permanent garrison whose job it was to keep down the turbulent Highlanders. During this time, the town which had grown up around the fort was called Maryburgh, after William III's queen. Only later was it changed to Fort William.

The West Highland Museum, in the town-centre, and well worth a visit, has historical, natural history and folk exhibits. These include a crofter's kitchen, early farm implements, jougs, the Marquis of Montrose's helmet (he fought an important battle at Inverlochy just outside the town), and a surveying instrument used apparently by Thomas Telford, the architect and engineer. Jacobite relics include several portraits and a bed in which Charles Edward Stuart, the Young Pretender, is said to have slept for a few nights after raising his Standard at Glenfinnan.

Fort William is a ideal tourist centre, standing at the hub of several roads. From the south comes the road from Glen Coe and Oban via the bridge at Ballachulish. This route into Lochaber offers a stunning combination of sea- and mountain-scape, especially for those who have driven north over the flat desolation of Rannoch Moor and then through the Pass of Glen Coe with its frowning

and beetling crags and mountains. Suddenly the landscape changes again. As you cross Ballachulish Bridge, an open bay on the left creates a wide vista across the sea-loch towards the mountains of Ardgour. Here is that subtle blend of scenery, of mountain and seascape, that is wholly West Coast. As you drive through Onich towards Inchree and the ferry to Corran, in Ardgour, the waters of Loch Linnhe sparkle tantalisingly through the trees.

Beyond the Corran ferry, the loch opens out again with fine views up the winding Conaglen to the high hills beyond. The old name for this upper part of the Loch Linnhe is *An Linne Dubh*, a shortened version of the original *An Linne Sheileach*, the second part of which means saltwater which is mixed with freshwater. Indeed, such is the rainfall in this part of Scotland that the burns and rivers of Lochaber regularly pump large quantities of freshwater into the sea-loch.

SPLENDID SCENERY

To the west of Fort William runs the Road to the Isles, the magnificently scenic road which closely follows the route of the West Highland Railway to Mallaig. Some would argue that this part of Lochaber is Scotland at her beautiful best, combining high mountain splendour with long, sinuous sea-lochs, eating their way like Norwegian fjords into the heartland of Lochaber. It's also a land of romance, heavy with history. Inverlochy, Fassiefern, Achdalieu and Glenfinnan, with their associations with Charles Edeward Stuart and Cameron of Locheil, all continue to cast their spell on modern travellers.

As you turn westwards from the Great Glen, you pass through Corpach. Look behind you

THE UPPER falls of Glen Nevis in early spring, swollen with snow melt. A number of years ago a scheme was put forward to harness the power of these waters for hydro electricity. Thankfully the ensuing outcry from lovers of this area put an end to that insensitive plan.

towards the high and might bulk of Ben Nevis, no doubt wearing its cap of cloud. In view of this king of mountains, many other ancient kings passed in days long gone. When Iona was the sacred isle of St Columba, many funeral proccssions from the north would come to Corpach, a place which means 'The Place of Bodies'. These ancient kings and chieftans would then be taken by galley from Corpach, down the length of Loch Linnhe, then across the Island of Mull to Iona and their final resting place.

From Corpach, out past the pulp-mill, you leave all signs of industry and development behind. The road runs straight along the length of Loch Eil before seemingly entering the heart of the mountains at Glen Finna, where the monument to commermorate Bonnie Prince Charlie's Raising of the Standard makes a foreground to the view of the head of Loch Shiel.

OPEN AND LONELY

North and east of Fort William, in the area once known as Brae Lochaber, lies a mass of high, rounded hills which contrast sharply with those shapely peaks of the west. The northern boundary of Brae Lochaber is the Corrieyairack Pass, between Glen Tarff and the headwaters of the Spey. Further south, this mass of hills stretches beyond Glen Spean to Loch Laggan in a long, wavy crest, culminating at Greag Meagaidh in Badenoch.

These hills, while perhaps lacking the sharply-etched features of the Grey Corries, the Mamores and the Aonachs to the south, nevertheless have their own character. They offer the hill-walker a different experience, being wide open and lonely, with some fine features such as the Parallel Roads of Glen Roy.

These extraordinary terraces, which line the hillsides on both sides of Glen Roy, are thought to be the successive beach levels of the ancient loch which once filled this glen, probably towards the close of the Ice Age. Three distinct terraces run along each side of the glen, those on the east side being more pronounced. The grass and bracken of the 'roads' stand out clearly against the heather-covered hillside.

In 1645, a forced march was made across these hills by Montrose's Royalist Army, from Fort Augustus in the north-east to Inverlochy, just north of Fort William, a march which preceded the Battle of Inverlochy in which the Royalist Army, under the command of the Marquis of Montrose, routed the Covenanting forces of the Duke of Argyll.

James Graham, fifth Earl of Montrose, and known in Highland Scotland in the seventeenth century as *An Greumach Mor*, was perhaps the greatest military figure thrown up by the Civil war. The key to his success was undoubtedly his association with Alastair Macdonald of Colonsay, known to his army of Highlanders and Irish gallowglasses as Colkitto, and one of the finest guerilla warfare exponents of his time. Many of Montrose's victories were more of an endurance test for his forces than proof of their fighting skills, and the combination of his leadership, Colkitto's influence and tactical brain, and the hardy toughness of his men proved successful time after time.

Having reached Fort Augustus on the banks of Loch Ness with his army, Montrose was given a message by one Ian Lom Macdonald, the Bard of Keppoch, (later to become Poet Laueate under Charles II, the first and last poet writing in the gaelic to be so honoured) that a large force, under the leadership of Archibald Campbell, Duke of Argyll, was chasing him northwards and was at that moment camped at Inverlochy, just north of the present town of Fort William. Montrose also knew that another large covenanating force was waiting to meet him at Inverness. it seemed that the Royalist Army was caught between two vastly superior forces.

HISTORIC HARDSHIP

It was then that Montrose and Colkitto showed their skill and bravery. With the Bard of Keppoch acting as guide, they marched their army over a tract of land the like of which no other army would have dared to cover, over the wintry, wind-scoured hills between the Great Glen and Glen Spean to outflank Argyll and take the Covenant Army by complete surprise. Sadly, the great Montrose was later betrayed by Macleod of Assynt in Sutherland, taken to Edinburgh, and hanged.

Modern hill-goers, thankfully, aren't under such pressure. Indeed, access to the mountains of Lochaber is generally straightforward. The best of the hills, the Ben, Aonachs, Grey Corries and the Mamores, can all be reached from Glen Nevis, a magnificent through-route which runs for 22 miles from Fort William to Loch Treig in the east.

A public road runs for six miles up the glen to a large car-park below the crags of Polldubh. From here, a superb footpath hugs the edges of a river-filled gorge of Himalayan aspect. It wanders through natural woodland, giving occasional glimpses of the huge Steall waterfall further on. After a while, at the top of the gorge, the scenery changes to flat meadowland, with high mountains all around.

As you follow the track onwards, the Grey Corries come into view on your left, with the high-tops of the Mamores on the right. Both groups of hills offer long, switchbacked ridges, with the Mamores probably just having the edge in popularity.

These high hills, and the wild and desolate country around them, really form the heartland of Lochaber. It's one of the finest and most popular hill-walking areas in the country, with upwards of 40 mountain tops, most of them Munros. From Ben Nevis, a magnificent arête of Alpine proportions, the Carn Mor Derarg arête, sweeps round the head of Coire Leis to Carn Mor Dearg itself at a height of 1,223 metres. Immediately westwards lie the twin tops of Aonach Mor and Aonach Beag, Lochaber's mountain anomaly, for Aonach Beag, the Small Ridge, is actually higher than Aonach Mor, the Big Ridge. But the Gaelic is quite correct, for the ridge of Aonach Mor is certainly longer and broader than that of Aonach Beag.

FINE RIDGES

From Aonach Beag, a rough scramble leads west to the start of the Grey Corries, a fine ridge of 10 major tops, Sgurr Choinnich Beag, 966 m, Sgurr Choinnich Mor, 1,095 m, Stob Coire Easain, 1,080 m, Stob Coire an Laoigh, 1,115 m, Caisteal, 1,104 m, Stob Coire Cath na Sine, 1,080 m, Stob a'Coire Leith, 1,105 m, Stob Coire na Ceannain, 1,121 m, Stob Choire Claurigh, 1,177 m, and Stob Coire Gaibhre, 930 m. Almost as an afterthought, a little way south of the main ridge, lies Stob Ban, a fine peak of 977 m.

South-west across the watershed of Tom an Eite, which surely must be the wettest place in Scotland, lies the long ridge of Sgurr Eilde Mor, 1,008 m, and the start of the mighty Mamores ridge. This 20kms ridge throws out ribs and spurs on both sides and makes a long, hard and magnificent day's outing. One or two minor difficulties are encountered en route, but any experienced hill-walker of better-than-average fitness should be able to complete the ridge in a day, starting either from the Water of Nevis side on the north, or from Kinlochleven in the south. The tops are Binnein Beag, 940 m, Binnein Mor, 1,128 m, Na Gruagaichean, 1,055 m, An Gearanach, 982 m, An Garbhanach, 975 m, Stob Coire a' Chairn, 981 m, Am Bodach, 1,032 m, Sgor an Iubhair, 1,001 m, Sgurr a' Mhaim, 1,099 m, Stob Ban, 999 m, and Mullach nam Coirean, 939 m.

While these ridges make grand undertakings in both summer and winter, and walkers can congratulate themselves after tackling either of them, their true significance is put into perspective when you can consider that several walkers have completed a round of Ben Nevis, the Aonachs, the Grey Corries and Mamores within 24 hours. Now, that's a bit more than your average stroll! The record for ascending, and descending, Ben Nevis is equally impressive, less than one-and-a-half hours. The average time for the ascent alone is about three-and-a-half hours.

Mallaig and Mallaigvaig, Lochaber

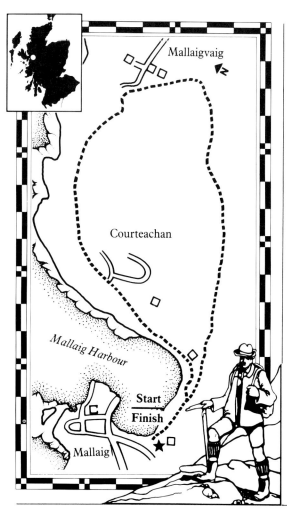

MAP: Ordnance Survey Sheet 34.

DISTANCE: 2½ miles.

ASCENT: 250 ft.

ACCOMMODATION: Youth hostel at Garramore, Morar. Hotels, guest-houses and bed-and-breakfast at Morar, Arisaig and Mallaig.

DIFFICULTIES: Nil.

Mallaig, at the end of the West Highland Railway line and a busy fishing and ferry port, is always a good place to be. In summer, the harbour heaves with visitors, passengers setting off or returning from the isles of Eigg, Rhum and Canna, or the Isle of Skye, or those just content to wander among the fish-lorries, peering down occasionally on the fishing-boats as the crews unload their catch or prepare for another trip. The continuous cry of gulls provides a background cacaphony, and there is an air of expectancy and excitement, and always something to look at.

ISLAND VISTAS

But there is also the knowledge that beyond the harbour wall is another world. Seaways lead to the Magic of the Isles, and beyond the headland the mountains of Knoydart rise high above the sparkling waters of Loch Nevis. A few hundred yards out of Mallaig, as you climb the hill beyond

the village, this other world opens up for you, a breathtaking scene which visitors to Mallaig shouldn't miss.

By the parking area at the south end of the harbour is a sign which says: 'Main road to East Bay. Old road Mallaigvaig, 50 minutes, 1½ miles. Pedestrians only'. Take the path between the houses and follow it for a hundred metres or so until it veers slightly to the left. A bench here offers a good view down on to the busy harbour. it's especially worthwhile sitting here for a while at night, when the lights of the fishing-boats bob around in the bay like fireflies.

Take the track again, and you'll soon notice the hills closing in on either side of you until you are walking through a small and narrow glen. This old track is the original access route for the people of Mallaigvaig, the hamlet which is our destination. After a while, you'll find it hard to believe that a busy fishing port is just behind you, but soon, as the hills open out as you climb higher, the views that are the attraction of this walk being to become evident.

The islands of Eigg, Rhum and Canna appear to the south-west, all three so different in shape and character. The finest in appearance is undoubtedly the Isle of Rhum, with the high-tops and pinnacles of its Cuillin hills bared sharp against the horizon. Further north is the Isle of Skye, with the Skye Cuillin appearing ragged and forbidding across the flatness of the Sleat Peninsula. Northwards, beyond the first of the

THE ROUNDED pate of Ben Nevis from Stob Ban. The round shouldered aspect of the mountain, although impressive in its sheer size, actually hides the true character of the mountain, the buttresses, ridges and crags above the Allt a Mhuillin to the north.

LOCH AN Eilean Castle, Rothiemurchus. Local legend claims that this was a lair used by Alexander Stewart, the Wolf of Badenoch but historians feel this is unlikely. His other castles were at Ruthven near Kingussie and Lochindorb, east of Grantown on Spey.

Above
ARLY MORNING on a
winter day. Loch
Lomond from Ben
Lomond. Loch Lomond
is one of the most
popular and best loved
lochs in Scotland. It is a
loch of great character
with its foot very much
in the lowlands and its
head almost choked off
by high highland peaks.

NEAR THE summit of
Ben Lomond with
the Arrochar hills in the
far distance. The climb
to the summit of Ben
Lomond is
straightforward, mostly
up a long broad ridge,
but from this point on
the scenery changes
dramatically until the
cliffs of the north east
corrie fall away at your
feet towards the small
farm at Comer.

HIGH ON the heights
of Ben Venue in the
Trossachs with Lochs
Achray and Vennachar
in the distance. This area
is one which has been
greatly romanticised by
the immortal pen of Sir
Walter Scott. This is the
land of The Lady of the
Lake and Rob Roy.

THE GLEN Coe peaks from the summit of the Buachaille Etive Mor. On the left of the obvious glen are the peaks and outliers of the Bidean nam Bian massif and on the right the jagged ridge of the Aonach Eagach.

Mallaigvaig houses, lies the entrance to Loch Nevis, and beyond it the dark hills and mountains of Knoydart.

Just as you reach the first of the houses, you may notice, on the right of the path, the stone wall outline of some old 'lazy beds'. This was an area which crofters used for cultivation, using a system of shallow trenches. The system allowed good drainage in areas with high rainfall, and invariably the trenches would be dug at the lower end of a field, where the excess water could flow away, as in this case, into a burn. The result of this 'lazy-bed' system can be seen today in the wave-like pattern on the surface of the field.

Follow the path around to where it joins up the main road, and follow it through Mallaigvaig and back down the hill into Mallaig.

This whole area is associated with the wanderings of Charles Edward Stuart, the Young Pretender, and it's claimed that on the stormy night of July 5, 1746, it was to Mallaigvaig that Prince Charles was brought by some Mckinnons following his fugitive travels in the Outer Hebrides and Skye. It was here that he stepped back on to the Scottish mainland.

The Glenfinnan Horseshoe, Lochaber

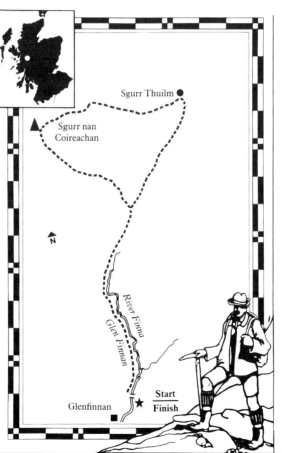

MAP: Ordnance Survey Sheet 40.

DISTANCE: 13 miles.

ASCENT: 4,600 ft.

DIFFICULTIES: A straightforward horseshoe ridge walk over rough ground. The biggest difficult is in descending from the summit of Sgurr nan Coireachan, which can pose problems in snow and ice conditions in winter.

ACCOMMODATION: Youth hostels at Fort William and Garramore. Hotels, guest-houses and bed-and-breakfast in Fort William, Corpach, Arisaig and Glenfinnan.

Here is Jacobite country, rich is historic association, legend and romance. At the head of the long and sinuous Loch Shiel, Charles Edward Stuart raised his Standard, at the spot where the clans gathered to begin their long 1745 campaign that was to end in tragedy, not only for themselves but for a Highland way of life that was to be no more. Months later, Charles returned to the area, but this time as a fugitive, spending a night out on Sgurr Thuilm itself.

A visitor-centre at Glenfinnan, run by the National Trust for Scotland, tells the story, but don't waste too much time on it. The hills await you, and this walk takes a full day.

This is an interesting corner of Lochaber.

SGURR NAN Coireachan, seen from the slopes of Sgurr Thuilm. The horseshoe walk follows the obvious ridge. To the north lies the wild lands of the Rough Bounds of Knoydart.

Other than this slim road from Fort William to Mallaig, no other roads penetrate a vast wilderness to the north, which includes the magnificently wild Knoydart area. Indeed, a round of Sgurr Thuilm, and its neighbour, Sgurr nan Coireachean, around the head of Coire Thollaidh, above Glen Finnan, gives a fine taster of the rough conditions found further north and west in the Rough Bounds of Knoydart themselves.

HARD WORK

Leave your car at the small car-park beside the A830 on the west side of the River Finnan, and walk up the private road, below the West Highland Railway viaduct. This impressive feat of engineering was finished in 1899. It was claimed that during the construction, a horse and cart fell into one of the hollow pillars!

After a couple of miles, a road branches off to the left to service the recently-built Glen Finnan Lodge, a modern construction that is very out of place in such a setting and makes one wonder just what kind of people are involved in local planning boards. Trying your best to ignore it, follow the road past Corryhully Bothy, which the SMC Munro guide describes as 'spartan'. That book was obviously put together before the estate did some work on the bothy, for it is now incredibly luxurious, and has even electric light and a heater!

The road ends at the stream which drains Coire Thoillaidh and Coire a' Bheithe, and just beyond it an obvious spur leads to the long ridge which is the Druim Coire a' Bheithe. This is where the hard work begins, head down and upwards over easy grassy slopes towards a small subsidiary top, and then north to the summit itself at 3,159 ft above sea level. From here the Knoydart hills fill the horizon to the north-west, fronted by remote Loch Morar. Behind you, to the north, is Loch Arkaig, and beyond it the Loch Quoich hills. Sgurr nan Coireachan fills the view immediately in front of you, at the end of a broad and knobbly ridge, splattered with tiny lochans and lined by old fence-posts.

From the summit of Thuilm, you'll have to descend south for a couple of hundred metres before continuing the traverse westwards. Enjoy the easy walking on this high and airy ridge. Some rocky outcrops offer easy scrambling, and the views are stunning. A lot of the ground is bare rock and the easiest route is undoubtedly along the crest of the ridge.

Sgurr nan Coireachan is slightly lower than Thuilm at 3,136 ft, but is a better summit. This Peak of the Corries is thrown up by a number of secret remote corries, craggy and wild and completely untouched by man. These are places where only the deer and the raven go, little gems of rock, heather and water, the bare elements that, mixed together, can be breathtaking in their stark beauty. I love this top. I love it, too, because it's not an anti-climax. The south-east ridge is steep and rocky and abuts on to some steep cliffs which fall down into Coire Thollaidh, a craggy and tumbling place of immense character. The ridge continues, in form and in interest, across the minor top of Sgurr a' Choire Riabhaich and down towards the River Finnan again. Drop off the ridge in an easterly direction to where a good stalkers' path skirts the foot of the crags to link up with the main Land-Rover track again. Return past Corryhully Bothy and back to Glenfinnan. It is a magnificent walk in superb country.

THE VERY fine bothy at Corryhully, complete with electric lighting. Many bothies, or open shelters, are maintained by the Mountain Bothies Association, a worthy organisation which should be supported by all Scottish hillgoers. Very few bothies have electric lighting.

Steall Glen, Lochaber

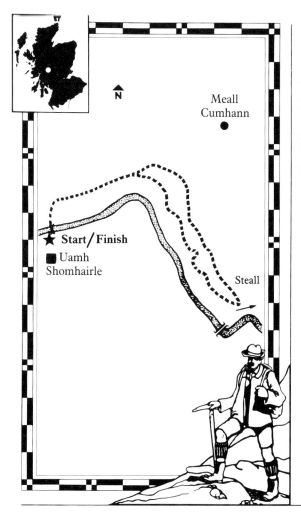

Start/Finish
Uamh Shomhairle
Meall Cumhann
Steall
N

MAP: Ordnance Survey Sheet 47.

DISTANCE: Three miles.

ASCENT: 200 ft.

DIFFICULTIES: Nil.

ACCOMMODATION: youth hostel and camp-sites in Glen Nevis. Hotels, guest-houses and bed-and-breakfast in Fort William.

Take your car up the length of Glen Nevis to the car-park at the end of the public road. Across the glen lie the steep slopes of Sgurr a Mhaim, with its quartzite cap, so often mistaken for snow, and in front of you the tree-clad slopes of Meall Cumhann. A 90-degree turn in the River Nevis pinches off the broad glen into a narrow gorge, through which the river tumbles and crashes. This walk takes you through that gorge and into a landscape of complete contrast beyond.

On the left-hand side of the car-park, the waters of the Allt Coire Eoghainn roar down the steep slopes from its hidden corrie above, creating a massive waterslide as the stream crashes down huge boiler-plate slabs. Many hill-walkers, bored with the tourist straggle on the other side of the mountain, climb Ben Nevis this way, but it's a long and steep ascent, apparently 1,220 metres at an angle of 35 degrees. That's tough walking in anyone's book.

The walk through the Nevis Gorge doesn't

demand the antics of a mountain goat, and a good footpath takes you all the way, although the drop below the path may in places be daunting to those unused to heights.

A signpost at the far end of the car-park indicates that a footpath runs to Corrour, 14 miles away. Corrour is a station on the West Highland Railway on Rannoch Moor, and another good footpath goes well beyond that, along by Loch Ossian, through the Bealach Dubh north of Ben Alder, and down to Dalwhinnie, via Loch Erichtside.

Follow the signpost, and the path, and you'll soon enter a delightfully mature wood of oak, pine, birch and rowan. From time to time, through the trees, you'll catch a tantalising view of what appears to be the head of the glen, with a great Grey Mare's Tail of a waterfall crashing down from the high slopes. This is the Steall Waterfall, and it plunges down the lower cliffs of Sgurr a Mhaim in one enormous surge of more than 100 metres.

Continue along the footpath as it winds through the woods. The crashing of the water in the gorge below will accompany you all the way, and soon the scene of that aquatic turmoil becomes apparent. As it flows down from the upper reaches of the Steall Glen, the River Nevis has worn a deep-cut, twisting channel through the very bedrock of the mountain. Through aeons of roaring and crashing, it's worn the rock into deep cauldrons and pots, and the scene is one at which to marvel.

But soon the dramatic course of the river changes. As you clamber over some boulders on the path, the scene changes from a jumble of rock, tree and water to an almost pastoral setting of flat meadowland. Only the crashing of the Steall Waterfall in the distance reminds you of the scene you have just passed through.

A wire bridge crosses the river to a tiny whitewashed cottage, once a croft, but nowadays owned by a local climbing club. It's a magnificent setting, with the river once again taking a right-hand bend into the broad glen which separates the Grey Corries from the Mamores. The route ends at Steall, before returning the way you came.

Just as you reach the jumble of boulders at the beginning of the gorge again, turn right and follow a faint track which zig-zags up the hillside. This offers a slightly different route back to the car-park, and, being higher, gives better views down the length of Glen Nevis and to the surrounding peaks. It involves a little more ascent, but is well worth it for the change of view.

THE STEALL Gorge, the boulders rounded and smoothed by the water action of aeons. It is amazing to think that the sheer power of water has worn down this gorge through the centuries. Watch it on a day of high spate and it becomes more believable.

Stob Ban, Mamores, Lochaber

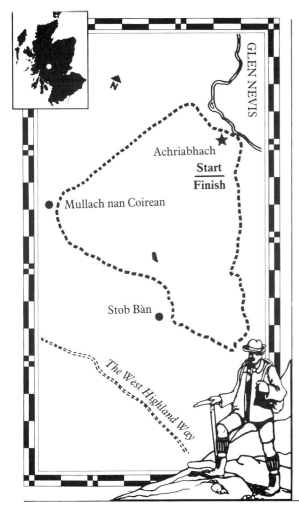

MAP: Ordnance Survey Sheet 41.

DISTANCE: 10 miles.

ASCENT: 4000 ft.

DIFFICULTIES: The ascent of Stob Ban is greatly enhanced in winter conditions, but only for those familiar with the techniques of using an ice-axe and crampons. The forest section above Achriabhach can be confusing. If in doubt, scream, put on a balaclava and mitts, and struggle through the undergrowth. Once safely at home you can become a member of the serried ranks of anti-Forestry Commission hill-walkers who loathe everything to do with modern conifer plantations.

ACCOMMODATION: Hotels, guest-houses and bed-and-breakfast in Fort William. Youth Hostel in Fort William and camp-sites in Glen Nevis.

One of the classic 'big walks' in Scotland is the traverse of the Mamore Ridge, 20-plus miles of high-level switchbacked ridge-walking which begins on Sgurr Eilde Mor, high above Kinlochleven, and finishes on Mullach nan Corean, above Achriabhach in Glen Nevis. This ridge-walk takes in 11 Munros, a good 'bag' for the keen collector, and gives a mountain experience which is second to none.

But such a walk requires stamina and fitness, and more often than not hill-walkers prefer to enjoy the Mamores in a number of shorter outings, taking in perhaps two or three of the tops at a time. This walk, to Stob Ban and Mullach nan Coirean, the most westerly of the range, offers more than just a taste of the Mamores. There is a great contrast in the two tops; one is craggy and rugged, with some fine buttresses and deep gullies, while the other is whalebacked and flat-topped, enclosing a number of rugged corries rimmed by grassy ridges. The views from Stob Ban back along the crest of the ridge is a rewarding one, while Mullach lifts you above Loch Linnhe with the great and impressive hulk of Ben Nevis just across the glen.

Start at Achriabach in Glen Nevis. You can park your car near the bridge above the gorge of the River Nevis. On a wet day in spring, this section of river is most impressive, with the swollen river fighting and crashing as it squeezes its way through the narrow, rocky defile. Across the bridge, a stile takes you into a field where a faint path indicates the route up into Coire a' Mhusgain. The path improves after a short distance and the walk up into this corrie is a superb one, passing through thin woods of oak and birch, and climbing higher to the sound of the stream crashing down its rocky course. All the time, the views beyond, directly down the length of Glen Nevis to the hills around Loch Arkaig, get better and better.

Soon the presence of Stob Ban is felt. Towering from its gradual northern ridge, it begins to dominate, with great scree runnels splitting the steep slopes into a complete system of buttresses, rocky and high, the topmost crags sparkling white in the sun, the effect not of snow, but of the amount of quartzite in the rock. Soon the path, which has been rising higher above the river, takes on a series of steep zig-zags which lift you higher on to the western slopes of Sgurr a'Mhaim. The temptation is to continue up those red screes, to bag this hill, because its summit feels and looks so close. Don't be tempted. The foreshortening effect gives a false impression, and the real rewards of Stob Ban are still to come.

CHANGING ROCK

The head of Coire a'Mhusgain is terrific. A lochan nestles below the steep contours of Sgor an Iubhair, the Peak of the Eagle, and red screes tumble down from the *bealach* which links it to Sgurr a'Mhaim. The track crosses the infant stream well below the lochan and zig-zags up to connect with the stalkers' path on the ridge. Already the views are opening up, down to Kinlochleven and the Glen Coe hills, and beyond Beinn a'Bheithir to the hills of Appin.

The path becomes rocky as it reaches the lip of Stob Ban's north-east-facing corrie. By this time, the stalkers' path, which is clearly shown on the OS map, is left behind. It runs round the south side of Stob Ban and dwindles out amid some rough scree. Continue up the north-east ridge to the summit and enjoy the views back along the length of the Mamores range, picking out the line of the ridge along the various peaks and humps of the tops themselves.

As you descend northwards and north-westwards, you'll notice a change in the rock beneath your feet as the grey and white quartzy rock of Stob Ban is replaced by a more reddish granite. Follow the rim of the north-facing corries, all looking towards Ben Nevis, as though bowing in obeisance, cross a subsidiary top, and then climb the final few hundred feet to the flat top of Mullach nan Coirean, the Summit of the Corries. The views south and west carry the eyes down the length of Loch Linnhe to the low hills of Morvern.

ROUGH DESCENT

Head north from the summit cairn and make sure you descend the correct ridge, the east ridge. There is an almost natural tendency to follow the north ridge, which will certainly take you down to Glen Nevis, but the forestry plantation which skirts this hill will chew you up and spit you out in pieces. The east ridge gradually swings northwards, too, and gives you a choice. As the ridge turns to the north, you can continue eastwards and down steep slopes and so avoid the forestry plantation altogether. You'll have a rough walk down beside the Allt a' Choire Dheirg, back to Achriabrach, but the path provides motivation by improving as you descend. The alternative is to follow the ridge right down to the edge of the forest, where a small cairn indicates a route through the trees to a forest drive.

NATURAL SIGNS

Now that's all very well if you can find the cairn, but it could be that a well-meaning person has kicked it down, or it may be covered in snow. In that case, follow the edge of the forest leftwards until you come to an obvious indentation. You find a stream running into the trees from here. Follow it, staying on its east bank, until you come across the forestry drive, which, in fact, stops at the stream. Follow the drive in a south-east direction, which will feel all wrong, but it soon zig-zags back to run north-west before turning east again to come out at the roadside at our starting place.

This walk can be reversed by taking in Mullach nan Coirean first, but it's a long, long haul up through the forest and then up to Mullach. Far better to enjoy the superb walk up by the Allt Coire a'Mhusgain first of all, and to suffer the consequences of modern conifer forests when at least you're walking downhill at the end of your day.

The Grey Corries, Lochaber

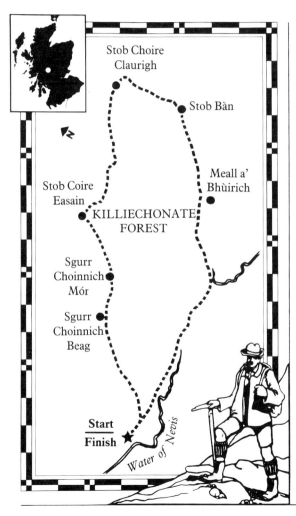

Stob Choire
Claurigh

Stob Bàn

Stob Coire
Easain

Meall a'
Bhùirich

KILLIECHONATE
FOREST

Sgurr
Choinnich
Mór

Sgurr
Choinnich
Beag

Start
Finish

Water of Nevis

MAP: Ordnance Survey Sheet 41.

DISTANCE: 16 miles.

ASCENT: 5,300 ft.

DIFFICULTIES: A long mountain walk with a long walk out at the end of the day. A long and serious walk in winter conditions.

ACCOMMODATION: Youth hostel and camp-sites in Glen Nevis. Bunkhouse at Achintee in Glen Nevis. Hotels, guest-houses and bed-and-breakfast in Fort William.

A walk through the Steall Gorge from the car-park in Polldubh in Glen Nevis never fails to impress me. It is a glorious half-mile which the author W. H. Murray once suggested was 'the grandest half-mile in Scotland . . . the nearest thing we have to a Himalayan Gorge'.

How accurate is that description. Where the Water of Nevis crashes down into Glen Nevis, in the area known as Polldubh, the ancient rock is scoured into great hollows and scoops, with natural woodland climbing to the precipitious, craggy slopes on either side. Now and then, as you traverse the narrow path which weaves its way through the woods, you get a glimpse of the Steall Waterfall, a real Grey Mare's Tail which thunders down into the Steall Flats. No wonder a group of conservationists fought hard a number of years ago to have this area kept natural. A hydro-electric scheme had been proposed, to harness the power

of the Steall Gorge waters. It would have meant defacing the base beauty of this spot, and something very special would have been lost for ever.

These thoughts went through my mind as I tramped up into Steall, heading for one of these awkward Munros that seem always to lie at the end of a limb. The limb in question was the Grey Corries, that fine ridge which teases out from the main Ben Nevis/Aonachs group. Away at its eastern end, like an afterthought, like Stob Ban, one of the hills I conveniently 'left for another day'.

The Grey Corries make up part of the superb panorama that holds the eye as you drive along the road from Spean Bridge to Roybridge in Nether Lochaber. And as you wander through upper Glen Nevis, past Steall, the undulating five-mile ridge reveals itself on your left. leave the Glen Nevis path just after the ruins of Steall, and climb quite steeply up the hillside making for the *bealach* between Sgurr a'Bhuic, an outlier of Aonach Beag, and Sgurr Choinnich Beag, the first of the Grey Corries tops. From here, it's an easy ridge-walk to the first Munro of the day, Sgurr Choinnich Mor, 3,603 ft.

Enjoy the view from here, south, overlooking the Mamore Deer Forest and beyond to the notched hills of Glen Coe, and north, across the Great Glen to the hills of Kintail, Glen Affric and distant Torridon. Ahead the Grey Corries ridge stretches away, switchbacked and tight, towards

APPROACHING STOB Choire Claurigh in the Grey Corries. This long switchbacked ridge is one of the classic high level walks in the area. Some hill walkers link it with a traverse of the Mamores in the south to make a super long distance traverse of Glen Nevis. For the fit only.

the last top of the ridge, Stob Choire Claurigh, and the ridge's little outlier, Stob Ban.

As I wandered along the Grey Corries ridge, head down on the map, so that I wouldn't inadvertently drop off the wrong ridge, I remembered why I hadn't climbed Stob Ban before. It's inconveniently placed, at the wrong side of an 800-metre *bealach*, and it's easy to miss it out, promising, in the optimism of youth, to come back to climb it another day. I seem to have collected dozens of these 'afterthoughts', and I'm now busy gathering them up. If I'd climbed them all at the right time, I would have finished the Munros long ago. What an affliction this Munro disease is . . .

The ridge between Sgurr Choinnich Mor and the next top, Stob Coire Easain, 3,545ft, is quite tight and airy, and in parts quite rocky. It's interesting walking. Beyond Easain, after you've climbed Stob Coire an Laoigh, the second Munro at 3,659 ft, the route undulates over several tops before beginning the climb to Stob Coire Claurigh, at 3,853 ft the final peak on the Grey Corries ridge proper. South of it lies Stob Ban.

At 3,217 ft above sea level, Stob Ban has often been likened to a slag heap, an unfair description in terms of scenic beauty, but apt in terms of underfoot conditions. While the main Grey Corries ridge is covered in quartizite, Stob Ban consists of shale, loose and unpleasant to walk on. I soon realised it was very much a case of three steps up and two steps down again. At one point I pulled up on a small outcrop and the whole lot came crashing down on top of me. I took a bit more care after that. It's a long way from anywhere on Stob Ban.

Getting to the top was a struggle, but well

THE NEVIS falls, at Polldubh in Glen Nevis. The walk from the car park at Polldubh to Steall is one of the classic walks of the area and has been likened to a walk in a Himalayan Gorge. It is certainly a walk to be recommended.

worth it, not only for the tick in the book, but for the wilderness quality of this summit. Southwards, the dumpy top eased into a long whaleback ridge, and it was alive with the sound of golden plover, always a delight. By now, the cloud had lifted and I was duly rewarded with far-flung views across the mighty Mamores to the south to the Glencoe hills beyond, and away eastwards to the purple swell of the Grampians.

It was a long trudge back down Glen Nevis to Polldubh, but, as usual, Steall Gorge weaved its magic spell and heavy legs were forgotten in its splendour. It's a great way to start and finish a day, and an inspiration for us to protect the beauty we have in the Highlands, if not for ourselves, then for our children.

Carn Mor Dearg and Ben Nevis, Lochaber

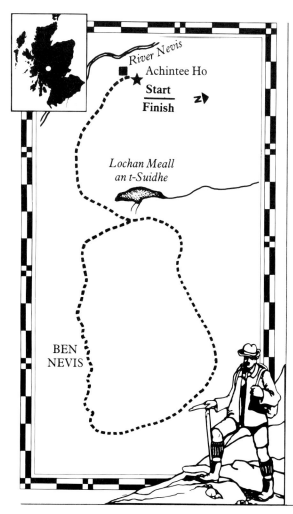

MAP: Ordnance Survey Sheet 41.

DISTANCE: 10 miles.

ASCENT: 5,300 ft.

DIFFICULTIES: More accidents occur on this hill, particularly in winter, than on any other Scottish mountain. Ben Nevis is serious in winter conditions. Note that well. In summer the walk outlined is rough but not exceptionally difficult. Beware of cornices above the north-east-facing cliffs which exist often until well into summer. Expect snow on the summit at any time of the year. I was once snowed-off a rock-climbing route in the middle of August.

ACCOMMODATION: Youth hostel in Fort William. Hotels, guest-houses and bed-and-breakfast in Fort William and surrounding villages. Camp-sites in Glen Nevis and a bunkhouse at Achintee.

The tourist track from Achintee, in Glen Nevis, to the summit of Ben Nevis, unless it is your first time and you nurture a strong desire to climb Britain's finest mountain by its quickest route, probably falls into the 'dull' category. From the south and west, the mountain is fairly dull, and hides its true character in the clench of its north-east-facing Coire Leis and the glen of the Allt a'Mhullin.

Sadly, most of those who climb Ben Nevis because it is 'the highest' never see any of the 'guts' of the mountain; but on reflection, perhaps they wouldn't want to. The north-east crags, buttresses, gullies and spires reflect a totally different impression of the mountain. This aspect shows a mean face, a demanding face, as one writer put it, and if I may repeat myself, of 'loveless loveliness'. There is little that inspires confidence in this array of cliffs, rather the opposite. Man realises his own stature, his own insignificance, his own immortality. He may come to tackle the huge faces, the ridges and the buttresses, in both summer and in the icy depths of winter, but he is never the conqueror – not on Ben Nevis.

From outside the Charles Inglis Clark Memorial Hut, beside the Allt a'Mhuillin, you gaze up at a complete array of cliffs, riven and torn by great fissures of scree into immense buttresses and long, tapering ridges. Not all the routes are difficult, some are no more than good scrambles, but these cliffs have a scale not found anywhere else, a seriousness that demands attention. It's this aspect that, in winter, draws mountaineers from all parts of the world. Ben Nevis's winter climbing is unique, and rarely easy.

To climb Ben Nevis without experiencing even a hint of what the north-east faces hold is like going to the beach and not seeing the sea. To thousands and thousands of hill-walkers and tourists, Ben Nevis is the sum of a long walk up a stony track in the company of hundreds of others, with little view and a pile of human graffiti in the shape of cairns and misplaced mementoes at the summit. The walk I'm going to describe not only climbs the hill, but takes you through some of the finest mountain scenery this country has to offer. The traverse of Carn Mor Dearg and its Alpine arête and on to the summit of the Ben is probably the most memorable way of climbing Britain's highest mountain. It is strongly recommended as one of the greatest walks described in this book.

ZIG-ZAGS

Start off on the tourist track at Achintee, on the east side of the River Nevis. Either that or cross the Water of Nevis by the bridge in front of the Youth Hostel in Glen Nevis and follow the track up the slopes in front to meet the tourist track. After about a mile-and-a-half, the track climbs up onto a broad *bealach* between Meall an t-Suidhe and Ben Nevis itself, a high, desolate area which cradles Lochan Meall an t-Suidhe. From here the tourist track starts a series of steep zig-zags, first southwards and then eastwards up the hill, but we want to carry on due north, over the *bealach* and then down into the glen of the Allt a'Mhuillin.

Already you'll be aware of the great cliffs to your right. Their very presence creates an atmosphere, ominous, almost overbearing, magnificent. Don't follow the Allt a'Mhuilin path eastwards, but, instead, drop down the rough, heathery slopes to the burn, cross it, and clamber up the rough, red granite slopes to the summit of Carn Beag Dearg, the Little Red Hill. The Big Red Hill, Carn Mor Dearg, is another mile or so along the ridge, which also crosses Carn Dearg Meadhonach. The crest of this ridge offers a splendid high-level traverse, with magnificent views across the glen to the real glory of Ben Nevis, the north-east-facing cliffs.

Carn Mor Dearg is a great vantage point for watching climbers on the classic routes, but the scale is so vast that you'll need good binoculars. At 4,012 ft, it's a big hill, but it seems swamped next to the bulk of the Ben. It's greatest feature is undoubtedly its arête, a high-level exposed ridge which connects the summit with the north-east ridge of Ben Nevis. After a couple of hundred yards, the arête narrows considerably to create what seems like a high-level tightrope composed of huge granite blocks. Nowhere is it particularly difficult, but the feeling of exposure is stimulating. A faint path just below the crest on its south-east side avoids any awkward sections, and gives you a vague feeling of security. The great feature of this arête is its beautiful curved sweep. It's perfect in its balance and symmetry, and delights the eye, particularly in winter when its graceful, shapely white curve contrasts with the deep blue of the sky.

CAREFUL NAVIGATION

But soon the graceful sweep of the arête merges into the bulk of the Ben itself, where a faint path picks its way upwards through a maze of giant boulders to the summit plateau. The summit of Ben Nevis is not one of my favourite places. Agreed, the view can often be incredible, as one would expect on the highest point in these islands, but the miserable ruins of the old Observatory, the hideous corrugated-iron mountain-rescue shelter, and the innumerable cairns and memorial stones that litter the place all stink of man's presence. Put these things together at sea level and the place would be declared a midden. Why is it different at 4,406 ft above sea level?

Take care with your navigation in thick weather as you cross the plateau. It's easy to become disorientated, and some very experienced mountaineers have found themselves descending too far south into the confines of Five Fingers Gully instead of the relative security of the tourist track, which will carry you comfortably back to the Lochan Meall an t-Suidhe and Achintee.

4. Torridon

THERE'S A HEART-STRUMMING sound to the very name of Torridon. It's emotive, an image of something unique, something special, something worthy of respect. As innocent adolescents, already daft on the hill-game, we would tentatively drop the name into mountain conversations. 'Torridon . . . Ah, yes, Torridon . . .', would be the dreamy response.

And the years have not lessened the impact of that name. Familiarisation has not taken the edge from it. It still prompts, a response from the heart. But why is the area so special?

Well, to understand anything about Torridon, you have to understand something of the nature of the beast. Within this area are some of the finest examples of Torridonian sandstone mountains to be found in a great belt of hills which range from Cape Wrath in the north, right down the western coasts of Sutherland and Wester Ross to Applecross and Loch Carron. Here the mountains themselves are beasts, leviathans which rise from sea level with long lines of mural precipice, rounded and terraced bastions topped by sharp-pinnacled ridges. Many of the summits are capped by grey Cambrian quartzite, which gives the impression that they are under a cover of snow the year round.

There's a breathtaking quality to the size and impact of these hills. Their terraced cliffs are cut at frequent intervals by long, vertical gullies, seams and joints on the infrastructure, which often form channels for streams and waterfalls, finishing lower down in great fan-shaped stone shutes.

And, strangely, the shapes of these hills are never the same. All are individual, idiosyncratic, primeval. All are rugged. Beinn Alligin is elegant, shapely, bejewelled. Liathach is monstrous and huge. Beinn Eighe is complex, a mini-range of peaks rather than one mountain.

While there is more to Torridon than mountains – and I'll come to that soon – it is the mountains that dominate. Between Glen Carron and Glen Torridon lie more than a dozen mountains thrown up from rough, loch-splattered moorland. This is the Bendamh and Coulin Forest, to which ancient stalkers' paths provide access to the walker from the south. These routes give an exhilarating approach to Torridon, and are highly recommended.

ROUGH CHARACTER

The real character of this area is best experienced by walking through it. The mountains form a compact group, but have individual shape and character, rising from rough and rugged moorland.

From Achnashellach railway station, in Glen Carron, a track runs up through the woods beside the crashing waters of the River Lair. Later I shall describe a walk which takes in the high tops of Coire Lair, but this route takes you through Coire Lair and through the Bealach Coire Lair and the Bealach Ban and so down to the head of Loch Torridon below the frowning bastions of Liathach.

The second route from the south crosses the Coulin Pass from Achnashellach to Loch Clair in Glen Torridon, a magnificent walk of a little more than seven miles, with superb views of Beinn Eighe and Liathach. And from Coulags, in Glen Carron, a right-of-way path runs below Maol Chean-Dearg all the way to Annat at the head of Loch Torridon. This path connects with the Coire Lair path at the watershed of Bealach na Lice.

POPULAR PEAKS

The Glen Torridon mountains are the peaks that people associate with this area, the previously described Beinn Alligin, Liathach and Beinn Eighe. The last are separated by a narrow glen, strangely named Coire Dubh (it's something of a local tradition to call the hill-glens corries), which connects with Coire Mhic Nobuill, which in turn separates the northern corries of Liathach from Beinn Alligin and Beinn Dearg. This glen, or coire, makes a magnificent through-route from the Diabeg road in the west to Coire Dubh, a fairly easy walk which takes you into the heartland of this remote area. The area is in the custody of the National Trust for Scotland, apart from the seven tops of Beinn Eighe which make up part of the Beinn Eighe National Nature Reserve run by the Nature Conservancy Council.

SLIOCH, THE Spear, rising fortress like from the still waters of Loch Maree, one of the great classic views of the Scottish Highlands. The route described in this book goes by way of a corrie on the other side of the hill.

These great mountains have often been described as being the oldest in the world. They were raised as a vast plateau 30 million years ago and carved into their present shape. It has been suggested that really they are no older than the Alps, at least in their present form. What is really ancient is the rock of the original chain, now exposed as the quartzite caps, are reckoned to be 600 million years old. The sandstone below them is even older, and the platforms of gneiss on which they stand are believed to be in the region of 2,600 million years old. These are, without doubt, the oldest rocks in Britain. No wonder, then, that they exude an air of primeval dominance.

At the western end of Glen Torridon is the tiny village of Annat, a few houses, a shop, a youth hostel and an information centre. From here the road climbs high above Loch Torridon, contouring the hillside and forcing a narrow route over bare country towards the hamlet of Diabeg. Here is another jewel of Torridon – a pier, a few cottages, pebbly beaches and a blue, sparkling bay, reflecting the frowning ramparts of the mountains above.

HIDDEN SPLENDOUR

Although the road stops here, the walker can continue to Red Point, near Gairloch, a superb clifftop ramble with, on a clear day, views across to the Outer Hebrides.

Most visitors to Torridon will probably arrive by car, through Strath Bran from Garve to Achnasheen, along by Loch a'Chroisg and over the Highland watershed at almost 1,000 ft, before dropping down the long, empty miles of Glen Docherty.

This glen is not one of Scotland's finest, with

little to hold the eye, but it's almost as though nature made it that way with a purpose: to capture your whole attention as the scene below breaks forth.

The first intimation of something special is the sight of Slioch, 3,217 ft, a majestic hill which rises virtually sheer from the waters of Loch Maree, one of the most splendid inland lochs in Scotland. As you continue down towards the green swards of Kinlochewe, you catch a view of a shoulder of mighty Beinn Eighe on your left, a hint of the magnificence which lies beyond.

SURVIVING FOREST

But Loch Maree calls for some attention. World-famous for its beauty (and, among fishermen, for its sea-trout), this loch typifies all that is held in the phrase 'Highland grandeur'. The largest loch north of the Great Glen, it covers 11 square miles, with a backdrop that is as incredible as those most ancient of ancient mountains to the south. And not only mountains, but the Caledonian pine forest which covers the slopes on the south shores of Loch Maree is pretty ancient, too, its generations of trees dating back 8,000 years. It's a wonder that the forest avoided the fate which befell other pinewoods in the Highlands, especially since local ironworks 350 years ago consumed 20 acres of oakwoods daily for charcoal. Even the wood above you, Coille na Glas Leitire, the Wood of the Grey Slope, was affected by the need for timber during the two World Wars.

These woods have been studied by the Nature Conservancy Council since 1951, and many of its findings can be seen in the Field Station at Anancaun, where the warden will give advice on

the nature trails which start from the picnic site at the lochside three miles north of Kinlochewe.

One of the most fascinating animals found in these woods, and increasingly in woods further south in the Highland, is the pine-marten. This magnificent animal was persecuted for centuries, and the continual destruction of its habitat, the pine forests, brought it close to extinction. Thankfully, it adapted to hill-country in Sutherland. The marten is long-bodied, about fox-size, with chocolate-brown fur and a yellow throat. It's tail grows to about a foot long.

The question is often asked why Kinlochewe (the Head of Loch Ewe) is so named. That sea-loch is some 15 miles to the west. Was it once connected to Loch Maree? Well, it seems that Loch Ewe was formerly also the name of Loch Maree. St Maelrubha came to Eilean Maruighe, one of the loch's islands, in the seventh century and made it famous as a place of pilgrimage. In time the loch was associated with the island, and the name of the island was corrupted to Maree, and so was the name of the loch.

Thanks to the faith of St Maelrubha, Eilean Maruighe became a holy shrine, and the place was apparently invested with holy properties. In 1772 the traveller Thomas Pennant visited the isle and wrote:

'The curiousity of the place is the well of the saint; of power unspeakable in cases of lunacy. The patient is brought to the sacred island, is made to kneel before the alter where the attendants leave an offering in money: he is then brought to the well, and sips some of the holy water; a second offering is made; that done, he is thrice dipped in the lake. The same

T HE SOARING slopes of Liathach in Glen Torridon, as seen from Loch Clair. For many these slopes appear as brutal and imposing, but the climb to the summit ridge is without any great difficulties.

operation is repeated every day for some weeks: and it often happens, by natural causes, the patient receives relief of which the saint receives credit'.

Either that or a bout of pneumonia . . .

Eilean Maruighe is one of 20 islands in Loch Maree, many of them covered in natural woodland. Eilean Subhainn is the largest, and even has its own loch with its own islands: islands on an island. As with Eilean Maruighe, there is evidence of former habitation on Eilean Grudididh, and on Eilean Ruaridh Bheag.

One of the nature walks from the NCC station at Anancaun, a circular walk of an hour or so, takes you 200–300 ft up the hillside to where you can gaze out over the pines and the loch to the bulk of Slioch, rising hugely above the water. Another walk takes you into the heart of the Beinn Eighe reserve at about 1,400 ft. Ahead lie the north-east corries of Beinn Eighe, full of light-coloured quartzite scree. Between the corries rugged moorland offers pasture to herds of red deer which in winter come down to shelter in the pinewoods. Up here, you may be lucky to see a golden eagle or wild-cat. Hill-foxes are common, and higher on the hill you'll see ptarmigan and raven.

Kinlochewe is well placed for touring Torridon. It has hotels, guest-houses, bed-and-breakfast establishments, and a caravan park, though this is for members of the Camping and Caravanning Club only. For the impecunious, there is a bunk-house.

Turn south at Kinlochewe and the road takes you past the lower slopes of Beinn Eighe to Glen Torridon itself. Several centuries ago this glen was thickly wooded, all the way from Kinlochewe to the sea at upper Loch Torridon, but all the trees were clear-felled, leaving only remnants of their former glory by Loch Coulin. The Nature Conservancy Council has planted trees here and there to break up the bareness of the hillsides, but the overriding feeling as you drive or walk through the glen is one of barrenness.

But the open hillsides do impress upon your mind the soaring slopes above, and it's difficult now to imagine Glen Torridon clothed in woodland. Leave your car at the car-park about two-and-half-miles west of Loch Clair and take the track to Coire Dubh, either round the great nose of Liathach into Coire Mhic Nobuil, or, better, round to Coire Mhic Fearchair on the north side of Beinn Eighe. It's on this side of the hill that you'll experience the real glory of Torridon.

Coire Lair Tops

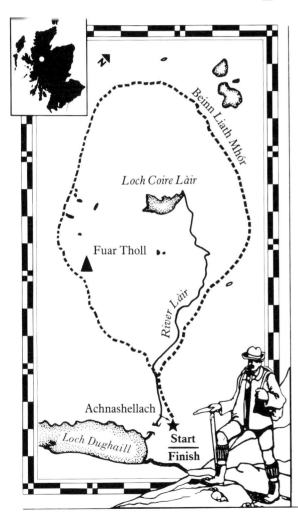

MAPS: Ordnance Survey Sheet 25.

DISTANCE: 10 miles.

ASCENT: 5,200 ft.

DIFFICULTIES: A long, hard walk which could be difficult in winter conditions. There is a good escape route from the Bealach Coire Lair.

ACCOMMODATION: Good bunkhouse at Achnasheen. Hotels, bed-and-breakfast and guest-houses at Glen Carron.

Pouring over a map of the Northern Highlands, I suddenly became aware that I'd been as guilty as most hill-goers of neglecting the marvellous country that lies south of Torridon and north of Strathcarron. More often than not, I'd thrashed on northwards towards the spectacular peaks of Torridon, or nipped over the Bealach nam Bo for the solitude of the Applecross Peninsula. It was time to put that to right, and to add a couple of new Munros to my list into the bargain.

Coire Lair, north-west of Achnashellach, is dominated by three splendid mountains: Fuar Tholl, the Cold Hollow at 2,975 ft; Sgorr Ruadh, the Red Peak at 3,149 ft; and Beinn Liath Mor, the Big Grey Mountain at 3,034 ft. A travese of these three tops around the skyline of Coire Lair is, as the SMC guide to the Munros almost understates, a rewarding walk.

Catching a settled period amid some appalling weather, I trundled up the moorland track from Achnashellach Railway Station. Trundled is perhaps the wrong term, but I find it difficult to find a suitable verb to conjure up the image of walking on such a boggy and soaking-wet track. It was about half-a-stride off swimming. Consolation came from the sheer majesty of the power of the various waterfalls, swollen with snow-melt and 48 hours' continuous rain. They absorbed my attention almost completely. Despite the underfoot conditions, I really enjoyed walking up through the pine-woods, and as I began to toil up the steep heather-and-boulder slopes of Beinn Liath Mhor's south-east top, my head was still ringing with the sound of roaring water.

It was good to stop here for a breather, and to appreciate the rest of the walk before me, over the craggy top of Sgorr Ruadh and above the long Mainreachan Buttress of Fual Tholl, a real climber's playground. The wind was by now tearing great rents in the cloud, and patches of blue sky were appearing all around. It was beautiful, but too cold to linger.

CAREFUL FOOTSTEPS

An undulating ridge of quartzite scree and moss leads to the summit, where the views of the Leviathan Torridon tops is superb. Take care on this summit, though, because you're likely to concentrate too much on the northwards view rather than where you're putting your feet, and a tumble on the sharp quartzite blocks hereabouts is likely to take its toll. Likewise, you have to take

F UAR THOLL, Sgor Ruadh and Beinn Liath Mor, the hills of the Coire Lair skyline walk. This walk from Achnasheen has become something of a modern classic and is a particularly challenging round in the depths of winter.

care on the descent to the Bealach Coire Lair, navigating through and around some steep crags.

From the *bealach* a faint path runs up over grassy slopes to a small lochan on the north-west ridge of the day's second peak. Sgorr Ruadh. From there it's a straightforward, if awkward, scramble on a scree-covered and rather steep ridge to the summit.

The next hill is Fuar Tholl, the smallest of the three, but the finest. Fuar Tholl is living proof that the whole Munro-bagging game is a nonsense. So many walkers come to Coire Lair and climb the two Munros only, leaving the best hill in the area for another time, post-Munro completion. It's a daft game, right enough, but I wasn't going to make that mistake. I've made it too many times in the past. Fuar Tholl is best climbed by taking its northern slopes head-on.

The mountain radiates three spurs, one north, one south and the other south-east, and it's on these spurs that the great rock features of the mountain are prominent.

HIGH WATER

Between the north and the south-east spurs lies the Mainreachan Buttress, a magnificent mass of terraced sandstone which seems to be suspended above a tiny lochan below the north face of the mountain. The rock-climbing here, according to many guidebooks, is among the best on sandstone anywhere in the country.

From the summit, I took an interesting line of descent, down the rim of the south-east corrie, a ridge which was tight and rather airy near the top. Soon I could scramble down to the lochan in the corrie, and then down the slopes back to the River Lair. I wanted to cross to the opposite bank to the

FUAR THOLL from Achnasheen. This is one of the three tops traversed in the Coire Lair skyline walk. Fuar Tholl is a popular mountain with climbers who enjoy magnificent sport on the Maireachean Buttress.

path, but the brown, peaty spate waters suggested I stay on the south bank. I didn't argue. I reached the railway line as the sky in the west exploded into a red-and-gold sunset. Great herring-bone clouds stretched across the sky, pink on the extreme edges, and becoming darker towards the middle. It was an extravaganza of nature, but this was no red-sky-at-night blessing. Next day we were back to the seasonal mixture of sleet, winds and grey.

Beinn Alligin

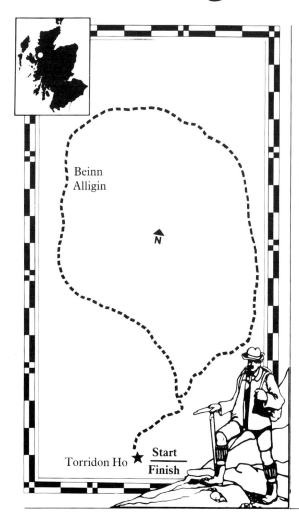

MAP: Ordnance Survey Sheet 24.

DISTANCE: Seven miles.

ASCENT: 4,000 ft.

DIFFICULTIES: Some scrambling involved if you keep to the crest of the ridge but a path bypasses the most difficult of it. A serious expedition in winter conditions.

ACCOMMODATION: Youth hostel at Torridon. Hotels, guest-houses and bed-and-breakfast in Torridon and Kinlochewe.

We'd pushed ourselves pretty hard the day before. Beinn Eighe and Liathach is a pretty big day by anybody's standards, and this morning we were feeling a little weary. But even as we procrastinated, wrapped cosily in eiderdown sleeping bags, the sun burst over the Sheildaig hills and we knew it had to be the day for Beinn Alligin.

The Torridon Triptych of Liathach, Beinn Eighe and Beinn Alligin must be one of the most magnificent groupings of mountains anywhere. It's also one of the oldest. Quartz-capped Torridonian sandstone offers an unusual mountain form, a landscape of ribs, buttresses and spires, intermingling with rounded battlements of immense bulk.

All three hills are big, and I mean Leviathan big – sprawling, prehistoric giants. Beinn Alligin is the Jewelled Hill, but it had failed to sparkle on

all my previous sorties. Heavy snow had robbed me of one ascent, and dank drizzle and mist, the usual Torridon diet, had given me a top but little in the way of a view. Today, it seemed, would bring the jackpot.

PRIMEVAL SOUNDS

Blue-tits belled as we wandered up through the fine old pine woods from the car-park alongside the Diabeg road, a path that runs up into the empty wilderness of Coire Mhic Nobuill. What a magnificent quarter this is. The path steadily gains height alongside the Abhainn Coire Mhic Nobuill, but after a while you have to leave it, cross the bridge over the river, and continue in a westerly direction up and into Coir' nan Laoigh.

As we tramped along the narrow track, so we were greeted by the lusty roar of stags in the prime of their rut. The day before we had listened and watched the primeval comings and goings, the sounds adding a real dimension to what is already a primeval and exciting place.

The effort of climbing the steep slopes up Coir' nan Laoigh is well rewarded by the view from the first summit, Tom na Gruagaich. As you come up from the confines of the corrie, the abruptness of the view stops you in your tracks. It's unexpected, so vast, superb.

On this day the whole of the Northern Highlands lay before us in crystal clarity. To the west was the Trotternish Ridge of Skye, and beyond it, dancing on a mirror-like sea, the hills of

B EAUTIFUL BEINN Alligin seen from across Loch Torridon from the south east. This hill well deserves its title of Jewel of Torridon. While the other Torridon giants are leviathon in appearance, Beinn Alligin has an appearance of subtle beauty.

Liathach

Harris and the low-lying shape of Lewis. To the north the coastline went on into purple infinity. Immediately in front were the Horns of Alligin. Then the three unusual peaks of the hill gave way to the thin wedge of Beinn Dearg, which in turn gave way to Beinn Eighe, which in turn gave way to a jumble of familiar shapes beyond Slioch. These are the hills of the Great Wilderness between Loch Maree and Little Loch Broom. We were breathless, not from the climb, but from the sight that lay around us.

The Alligin ridge now lay before us. A careful descent from Tom na Gruagaich, and a steepish climb brought us to the real summit of the mountain, Sgurr Mhor. Just here, below the summit, the cliff is split by an immense rockfall of cataclysmic proportion. The rubble of it lies in the corrie floor below, a testament to the mighty power of nature.

After Sgurr Mhor, the challenge presented by the Horns of Alligin was taken up, a trio of sandstone pinnacles which can be scrambled over, or bypassed by a track on their south side. We did a bit of both. Bess, my canine pal, isn't too fussy about scrambling, which is understandable, since she has four legs to contend with. So we compromised: some easy scrambling, and some easy walking, over the horns, off the ridge, and down across the moorland back to the Abhainn Coire Mhic Nobuill path.

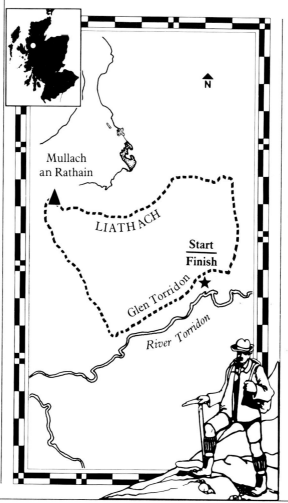

MAP: Ordnance Survey Sheet 25.

DISTANCE: Seven miles.

ASCENT: 4,000 ft.

DIFFICULTIES: This is a walk for the experienced mountain-walker. The Am Fasarinen Pinnacles should be attempted only by experienced scramblers. Even the path which avoids them is exposed and can sometimes be difficult to locate in thick weather.

ACCOMMODATION: Youth hostel at Torridon. Hotels, guest-houses and bed-and-breakfast in Torridon and Kinlochewe.

Some years ago, I sat on a high sandstone block on the south side of Glen Torridon and gazed across the gulf of the glen towards the vast, grey bulk of Liathach. I remember feeling overwhelmed and oppressed by the size, bulk, and steepness of the hill. It frightened me. I can't explain why, but in those moments I developed a healthy respect for that mountain . . . The Grey One . . . I felt it was well named.

It was another couple of years before I climbed it for the first time. I chose a clear day in early winter, when a hard frost had Torridon in its grip. I had enjoyed the drive north, through Garve and Achnasheen, and Slioch basked in the early -morning sun. As I turned down Glen Torridon from Kinlochewe, past the broad slopes of Beinn Eighe, I was suddenly confronted again by

Liathach's overwhelming bulk. But this is more than just one mountain. Like neighbouring Beinn Eighe, this hill embraces a whole range of peaks. A five-mile ridge, thrown up from steep slopes of tiered sandstone, runs along the north side of the glen, reaching its climax in a fine, bold peak, fronted by a great blunt buttress.

ROCKY STEPS

The belly-roars of rutting stags filled the still air as I left the car in the glen half-a-mile east of Glen Cottage and took the track which climbs up to the hanging hollow of Coire Leith. This route misses the eastern tops of the hill, but takes in the two Munros of Spidean a'Choire Leith, 3,456 ft, and Mullach an Rathain, 3,358 ft.

Higher up the hill, cairns mark some zig-zags which cross rocky steps, heather and steep grass and lead over a break in a rock band which seems to cross the face of the mountain. It's a steep scramble into Coire Leith, where a scree gully gives access to the ridge between Bidean Toll a'Mhuic and the summit boulder-field of Spidean a' Choire Leith. Spidean is the highest top of the mountain, and the views on a good day are extensive, all the way from Ben Hope in the north to Ben Nevis in the south. Even more spectacular is the ridge ahead to the summit of Mullach an Rathain. This 2 km ridge is extremely narrow and for much of its length is broken and shattered into a series of spectacular spires, the Fasarinen Pinnacles.

These shattered sandstone teeth fall away dramatically into Coire na Caime on the north side, one of Liathach's magnificent corries which are hidden from the tourist in Glen Torridon. Really to catch the splendour of this mountain, you have to traverse it, or admire it, from the relative remoteness of Coire Mhic Nobuill in the north.

A scramble across the summits of these Fasarinen Pinnacles is far from impossible, and the hill-walker who has a head for heights and some experience of rock-climbing will love the airy traverse. Others will be advised to follow an exposed, but well-trod footpath which hugs the south side of the various pinnacles and buttresses and leads to the second Munro of the hill, Mullach an Rathain, the Summit above the Horns.

A wide, grassy ridge carries you on to the summit, and the OS Pillar. To the north, a short, stony arête runs out to the highest of the Pinnacles and the lower peak of Meall Dearg, again overlooking the wonderful Coire na Caime.

A long ridge runs westwards down to the subsidiary top of Sgorr a Chadail, with fabulous views across Loch Torridon, but the descent route goes westwards and south of the summit cairn, a narrow ridge dropping towards a broadening slope of broken, scree-filled gullies and worn terraces, and down towards the road alongside the Allt an Tuill Bhain. It's then only a short walk back to the car beyond Glen Cottage.

Beinn Eighe

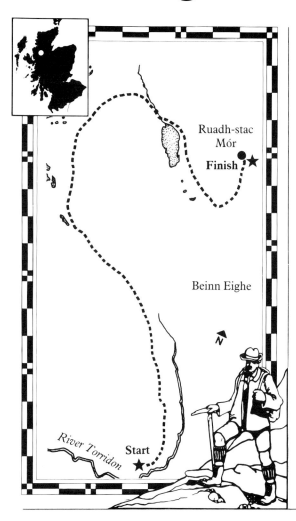

MAP: Ordnance Survey Sheets 19 and 25.

DISTANCE: 12 miles, there and back.

ASCENT: 2,800 ft.

DIFFICULTIES: A straightfoward walk, though the climb on to the main ridge can be laborious due to scree. This is probably the easiest way on to the summit of Beinn Eighe. The walk to Coire Mhic Fhearchair is a fine low-level alternative and a grand walk in its own right.

ACCOMMODATION: Youth hostel at Ledaig, Torridon. Hotels, guest-houses and bed-and-breakfast in Torridon, Kinlochewe, Gairloch and Inverewe.

While Liathach is oppressive and Leviathan in form, Beinn Eighe is shapely and attractive, from her whited-capped quartzite summit peaks to her more benevolent easier-angled slopes. While Liathach is butch and broad-shouldered, Beinn Eighe suggests femininity, hence the female gender.

But the problem with such anthropomorphism is that it can lead you into deep trouble, especially in these days of radical equality. Dare I say that Beinn Eighe is a complex mountain, with a difficult side to her character, and with long scree slopes which are disheartening and tiring, to say the least? In an attempt to save face, let me describe a route which avoids most of the complexity and the awkward treadmill scree chutes, a route which shows off the remarkable features of this hill in what is a fairly easy and straightfoward hill-walk.

But first, the facts. Beinn Eighe is another of those mountains which is actually a small range with a collective name. Lying just south-west of Kinlochewe and Loch Maree, it is separated from Liathach by the dramatic Coire Dubh. It has seven peaks higher than 3,000 ft and a clutch of remarkable north-facing corries, of which the best, Coire Mhic Fhearchair, is arguably the most impressive corrie in Scotland. With its lochan reflecting the high sandstone tiers of the Triple Buttress, it has the awesome atmosphere of some great cathedral, especially on a day which is quiet and hushed.

The traverse of all the tops is a long expedition, but this route to the actual summit of the mountain, Ruadh-Stac-Mor, 3,313 ft, has the advantage of taking in Coire Mhic Fhearchair along the way, or even treating the corrie as a destination in itself as a relatively low-level walk. Just recently I wandered round Coire Dubh and up into the corrie with my family, who felt the effects of a very hot day. While they enjoyed a picnic and a paddle in the lochan, I pushed on up the slopes to Ruadh-Stac-Mor and back before joining them for the return to Glen Torridon. It was a good day for all.

The starting point is the car-park by the A896 in Glen Torridon, just west of the Allt a' Choire Dhuibh Mhoir. A signpost points out the route, and the path is worn and obvious as it takes its

THE TRIPLE Buttress of Coire Mhic Fhearchair, Beinn Eighe. The route to the summit, as described in this book, takes some steep scree slopes well to the left of the Triple Buttresses. This corrie is one of the finest in all of Scotland.

course up into Coire Dubh Mhor, round past the eastern ramparts of Liathach. As you progress through Coire Dubh Mhor, which is really more of a pass than a corrie, you'll become aware of the majestic and spectacular northern corries of Liathach. What a contrast to the huge, peeling flanks of the south.

THE GRAND HALL

Once past the obvious watershed, beyond a small lochan, a path peels off to the north round the great prow of Sail Mor. Follow it around, enjoying the views into this great tract of wilderness country, the home of red deer and eagle. Soon the path begins to climb again, past some waterfalls and finally up into the grand hall of Coire Mhic Fhearchair itself. You'll be in no doubt as to why this is one of the great mountain scenes in Scotland.

The route to the summit of Beinn Eighe's highest top is now straightfoward, though awkward in terrain terms. Ruadh-Stac-Mor is the end-point of the ridge to your left, the eastern arm of Coire Mhic Fhearchair. Cross the outflow of the lochan and make your way round its east side. A path of sorts weaves its way through heather and jumbled boulders. Ascend the rough slopes towards the obvious col which separates the top from the main ridge of Beinn Eighe, and from there you'll find it an easy walk over quartzy screes to the summit.

Slioch

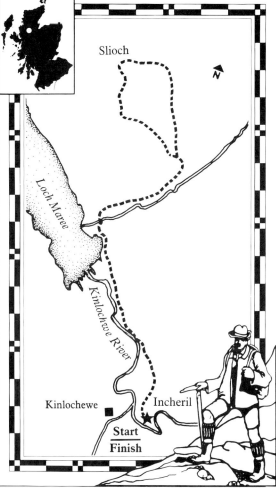

BEINN EIGHE from the Coulin Pass. This ancient right of way makes a magnificent entry to the land of Torridon and beats arriving by car any day.

MAP: Ordnance Survey Sheet 19.

DISTANCE: 11 miles.

ASCENT: 3,600 ft.

DIFFICULTIES: A magnificent walk in stunning surroundings. No real difficulties, although the slopes above Coire Tuill Bhain could become avalanche prone in certain winter conditions.

ACCOMMODATION: Hotels, guest-houses and bed-and-breakfast in Kinlochewe, Poolewe, Shieldaig. Youth hostel in Ledaig, Glen Torridon.

Slioch, the Spear, is a real fortress of a mountain. Just how relatively impregnable it was I found out one day when several of us drove north in search of sunshine, or at least in search of an escape from the dreich wet and windy weather we had experienced the day before on the Monadhliath hills in Speyside.

New Year's Day, in my experience, is invariably dreich, but it has nothing to do with alcoholic over-imbibing – or not usually. An escape to the hills is my invariable answer. A long walk-in to Carn Dearg and back to Newtonmore in just as few hours gave us the exercise and fresh air we wanted, but didn't offer much in the way of far-flung views or crisp underfoot snow conditions, the ideal combination for a winter day's hill-walk. But the BBC weather man at half-past six gave us some hope. Atlantic troughs would be blowing across the country from the south-west, bringing drizzle and low cloud. Most of the country would be affected. But then, almost as an afterthought, or because he had a bit of time to spare, he briefly mentioned that north-west

Scotland would probably escape the troughs and would be sunny.

Clutching that scant bit of optimism like a drowning man grabs on to a lifebelt, we left Speyside early next morning and arrived in Kinlochew, near Loch Maree, about half-past eight. It was still dark, but here and there a star shone from a brooding sky.

We parked the car at Incheril, a group of cottages and farm-buildings about half-a-mile east of Kinlochewe, and tramped along the three-mile walk-in by the Kinlochewe River. As we turned away from the south-east shores of Loch Maree, and began to climb up into Gleann Bianasdail, the sky above the big mountains of Torridon across the loch began to turn shades of red and pink.

Soon we could see the sunshine burst on the top slopes of hills above us, picking out every gully and buttress in clear, bright relief. The weatherman had been right. It was going to be a good day, and it was, one of the best.

BROKEN DEFENCES

Slioch, this improbable giant of Torridonian sandstone which dominates the north shores of Loch Maree, is violently steep on three sides. But a great corrie, the Coire Tuill Bhain, or White Hollow, carves into its eastern extremity and offers a break in its defences. And today it lived up to its name, for it was a white hollow, and, even better, good, hard new snow filled the short gullies up on to the hills's main ridge.

The views from Slioch are wonderful. The Torridon hills stand out in bold relief: Beinn Eighe, appearing more as a range of mountains than a single peak; Liathach, seen from its better side, as opposed to the regular view from Glen

Torridon; and Beinn Alligin, strung out like the beautiful jewel of Torridon that it is. From the summit, the eyes are led naturally past the island-studded length of Loch Maree to Poolewe and beyond, where the long Trotternish peninsula of Skye lies on a blue horizon, and then round to a feast of wilderness mountains, those peaks of the Great Wilderness itself, that jumble of hill and glen, peak and mountain that makes up this area between Loch Maree and Little Loch Broom.

By this time the sun was shining boldly, and to our right, in the east, a great line of cloud separated the good weather from the bad. We felt priviliged to be where we were, even blessed. It had been a long walk to the summit of Slioch, after the long walk of the day before, but it's amazing how stiff limbs can be soothed by some sunshine and snow. We returned to the car at Kinlochewe in a blaze of sunset colours, the finest I've seen in years. And yet, on the way home as we stopped to fill up with petrol at Achnasheen, the attendant looked at me as if I was daft when I mentioned it had been a wonderful day.

'See that line of clouds in the sky over there?' he asked.

I nodded.

'Well, the other side of that line may have seen wonderful weather, but this side has been grey and freezing-cold all day'.

It's worth listening to the chance remarks at the end of a nation-wide weather forecast . . .

5. Ullapool Area

THE ANCIENT NORSE called this place Ulli's Steading, an oasis of softness amid dramatic, rugged scenery. Stop in your car at the top of Corry Point, on the Braemore to Ullapool road, and gaze down on the village, Freshly-imprinted on your memory will be the bareness of the Dirie Mor, the land around Loch Glascarnoch, the high, bald neighbours of Beinn Dearg rising from the distant moors on one side and the distant Fannichs on the other. No doubt the jagged spires of An Teallach will have attracted your attention, too. But, suddenly, the scenery changes as you descend towards Loch Broom. Forests, woodland and an abundance of rhododendrons soften the scene, as do the spacious parks at the head of the loch. The contrast is as remarkable as the first view of Ullapool is surprising.

A gentle bay eases its way round to a point which juts into Loch Broom, beyond which lies the shadow of the low Summer Isles. Beyond them are the Hebrides. Along the south shores of that bay huddle the town buildings, glistening white in the light. A long pier is the focal point, where most of the buildings congregate, while others lie back, massed behind and beyond the pier.

The Norse chose wisely. The place is well sheltered. Indeed, palm trees grow in the gardens, and the site of Ulli's Steading was a late Ice Age beach 50 ft above the level of Loch Broom. it was a good trading position, and good for fishing, too, and it was fish that were to provide a salvation for this place in later years.

In 1788, the British Fisheries Society founded what is the present town of Ullapool. Its birth then, and later its prosperity, was owed entirely to herring. For almost 40 years the Loch Broom herring industry was famous. A *Statistical Account* of the eighteenth century remembers the scene:

'People are instantly afloat with every species of seaworthy craft. They press forward with utmost eagerness to the field of slaughter – sloops, schooners, wherries, boats of all sizes are seen constantly flying on the wings of the wind from creek to creek, and from loch to loch, according as the varying reports of men, or the noisy flights of birds, or tumbling and spouting of whales and porpoises attract them'.

In those days, unlike today, the herring shoals could be relied on. They passed Loch Broom from May to September, with prodigious shoals swimming into the loch itself. Local boats would place their nets at the mouth and fishing stations were set up on Isle Martin, at the mouth of Inner Loch Broom, and on the Summer Isles. But the resultant overfishing had a marked effect. The shoals dwindled, and by 1880 the herring had vanished.

This 50-year herring boom brought about the formation of the British Fisheries Society, which had began to build Ullapool as a permanent fishing station, with a large pier, sheds and housing for the fishermen. Many of the houses survive to this day.

But fishing picked up again, and the place thrived, especially once the tourist industry began to take shape. Today, Ullapool is a lively, bustling town, an embarkation point for the car-ferry which leaves daily for Stornoway on the Isle of Lewis. It is also a popular sea-angling centre. But probably more than anything else, Ullapool is perfectly situated for walkers and others wishing to explore the unique countryside of the far north-west, those magnificent areas of Coigach and Assynt and their remarkable mountains.

But let's backtrack a little, east and south of Ullapool. As you leave the Dirie Mor behind you, and reach the road junction at Braemore, instead of dropping down Strath More to Ullapool, turn left on to the narrow, winding Feighan road. The next 14 miles to Dundonnell, and the walk to the mighty An Teallach, are unforgettable.

FAMINE YEARS

This is the so-called Destitution Road, named because it was constructed during the famine years of 1847–48 as a means of providing work and food for the stricken crofting populations of the West Coast, facing hardship after the glory years of the herring industry. When the herring vanished, the local economy collapsed and times

AN TEALLACH from the south, from Beinn Tarsuinn. The castellated skyline is made up of the Corrag Bhuidhe Buttresses and Sgurr Fiona. An Teallach means The Forge and it is undoubtedly in the top five favourite mountains of most hillgoers.

were evil.

'Destitution Road' is an unfortunate name, for the road and the scenery is marvellous. In front and to the left are the high hills of the Fannich deer forest; to the south, the twin spear-points of Slioch on Loch Maree-side; and then, as you turn west again, just beyond Loch a'Bhraoin, the spiry ridges and pinnacles of An Teallach appear ahead of you.

FINE CHOICES

Now you are on a high, boggy moorland. Only the livid-white skeletons of trees, half-buried in the peat, remind you that this area was once covered in pine trees, part of the ancient Forest of Caledon. A drove road once crossed here, and the old Feighan House was once an inn for the drovers.

Beyond the summit, the road drops steeply, down through birch-woods, with some fairly tight twists in the road. An Teallach appears again through the trees, closer now, in full grandeur. Just beyond lies Dundonnell, on the shores of Little Loch Broom.

The climb to the summits of An Teallach is a fine one, but so to is the walk south beyond the great cirque of Loch Toll an Lochan towards Shenavall and the wilds of the Great Wilderness, a massive area of high, remote mountains. This estate was once known as the Whitbread Wilderness, after its owner, Colonel Whitbread, who was keen to discourage walkers and climbers. In many ways he did us a great service, for the area is comparatively unspoiled and unused. It's a wonderful place.

But back to Braemore . . .

Stop, if you can, to visit the Corrieshalloch Gorge. This is a spectacular mile-long, 200ft-deep schist-eroded gorge into which drop the Measach Falls. Imagine, if you can, the mountains behind you covered by an ice-cap several thousand feet thick. From this ice-cap great glaciers flowed slowly west to the Atlantic, grinding and scouring, smoothing and striating the very bedrock. But later, when the ice-cap began to melt, great rushing streams were formed, and in time the water which crashed down towards Loch Broom cut this massive gorge from the solid rock.

The falls can be viewed to best advantage from an observation point and footbridge above the gorge. Watch the River Droma below you explode from the chasm above and plunge down the falls. Both sides of the gorge are covered with dwarf rowan, birch, hazel and alder, a rich undergrowth. The area has an uncommon lushness, and the footpath above passes through woods of larch, pine and holly, with some oak and sycamore. The area is protected by the National Trust for Scotland, which has provided car-parks by the road.

Two miles further north, the Lael Forest Garden is also worth a visit. It contains about 150 different trees and shrubs from many parts of the world, and some good forest-walks offer fine low-level alternatives to the tops in poor weather.

Ullapool also provides some good alternatives from striding the high tops. A boat trip to the Summer Isles is well worth while. These are scattered, sparsely inhabited islands, but superbly atmospheric, with an abundance of sea-birds. The great environmentalist, Frank Fraser Darling, once lived on the largest of the islands, Tanera Mor, and it was here that he wrote one of his best books, *Island Years*.

Driving north from the town, you enter another world, away from the softness of Ulli's Steading to a world of upheaved mountains, the bare bones of the earth showing through its thin, peaty skin. Beyond Ardmair Bay, across the waters of Loch Kanaird, the long ridge of Ben More Coigach hides the complexities beyond, but the road drops and twists around the head of the loch, past white croft-houses and crags, and soon the real Coigach reveals itself on your left.

This Coigach is the Place of the Fifths, from the ancient Celtic tradition of dividing land into five parts. Here is a wilderness indeed. Hundreds, if not thousands, of lochans lie scattered across the bare moorland, and the mountains rise in almost monolithic isolation. Stac Pollaidh and the hills beyond are particularly primeval in appearance.

The main road north from Ardmair continues into Sutherland, but at Drumrunie another road, single-track, branches off to the left. Follow it, with the peaks of Ben More Coigach on one side and Stac Pollaidh on the other. Pass by the mountains for the moment and continue to Achiltibuie.

BEAUTIFUL BAYS

Pass Achnahaird, with its half-mile of salt-flat, where you can watch flocks of dunlin and ringed plover feeding, and continue south to Badentarbat Bay. The bay is protected from the vagaries of the Minch by the cluster of the Summer Isles, which seem from here to lie close to the shore. The hamlet of Achiltibuie is stretched over some three miles of the bay, and has a church, hotel, shops and a pier. Beyond the village, a shoreline path runs to Strath Kanaird below the steep escarpment of Ben More Coigach.

BEINN a'Bheithir, above Glencoe village and Loch Leven.

LOOKING across to Loch Lurgainn and Coigach from Stac Pollaidh. Stac Pollaidh offers an easy walk to this point but to reach the real summit of the mountain you have to tackle some big sandstone pinnacles. Good scrambling for those so inclined.

EVENING ON the slopes of Eididh nan Clach Geala, near Beinn Dearg. This photograph was taken in early January when unseasonally mild temperatures made it feel like a summer's afternoon.

THE Matterhorn aspect of Suilven from Elphin. You can either walk in to the hill from here, climb it and return the same way, or you can traverse the mountain and continue to the village of Lochinver on the west coast.

THE PEAKS of
Coigach across
Loch Lurgainn. These
little mountains have a
fine character and are
well worth exploring. A
comparatively few
number of people go
there, most preferring
the more popular route
on Stac Pollaidh.

Beyond Achnahaird, a branch road continues for a mile-and-a-half up the coast to Reiff. This is a grand coastline, with a sandy bay, a splattering of boulders and low sandstone cliffs. Rock-climbers enjoy some difficult, if short, problems on these cliffs, and along the tops the walking is magnificent on bare slabs and short turf. Deep chasms thrust far into the land, forming long and sinuous caves, many of which are well worth exploring.

RESERVED BEAUTY

North of the Achnahaird-Drumrunie road lies the breathtakingly beautiful Inverpolly National Nature Reserve. Looked after by the Nature Conservancy Council, this is a remote and wild confusion of moors, burns, lochs and high, isolated peaks – Cul Mor, 2,787 ft, Cul Beag, 2,523 ft, and Stac Pollaidh, 2,009 ft. Just outwith the Reserve, in the north, lie the dramatic peaks of Suilven, 2,399 ft, and Canisp, 2,779 ft. It is an area no one should miss.

A short introduction to the reserve is the low-level walk which takes you into the heart of the wilderness to Loch Sionascaig. Leave the road a few hundred yards east of the cottage of Linneraineach, and a short climb takes you over an obvious *bealach*, followed by a long descent to some birch-woods above a great, water-filled valley. Turn left down the banks of the Gleann Laoigh Burn, a lovely stream fringed by trees and bright-green turf. Continue to Loch Gainmheich, where the river flows into a wide, sandy bay. At the far end of the loch, pass a keeper's hut and cross a plank-bridge near Loch Scionascaig to join the track which runs back to Loch Lurgainn. Watch out for greenshank and black-throated

AN TEALLACH, from left to right, the Corrag Bhuidhe buttresses, Sgurr Fiona, and Bidein a Ghlas Thuill. A complete traverse of this fine mountain is a magnificent trip and one that is to be highly recommended.

divers. Red deer herds roam this interior, and you could well spot golden eagle. The lochs reflect the tall towers of the Inverpolly peaks, but there is no feeling of being dwarfed by them. The mountains stand well back, and the skies are open and wide.

The landscape has a gentle subtlety, with lush, grassy slopes giving a softness not associated with these areas. But that is one of the attractions of this whole area. It has more variety than any other area in Scotland. On a good day, it's not too far from perfection.

THE SOUTH western crags of Cul Mor from the shores of Loch an Doire Dhuibh. There is a wildness and remoteness to this whole area which is unique. The mountains rise clear from the bare mattress of moorland and each has its own peculiar character.

SGURR FIONA, right, and the pinnacles of An Teallach. Sgurr Fiona was recently uprated to Munro status and so there are now two Munros to bag on An Teallach, this one and the highest top, Bidein a Ghlas Thuill.

An Teallach

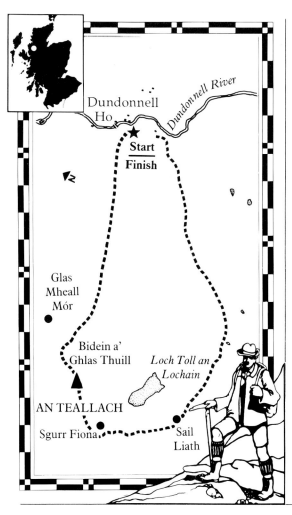

MAP: Ordnance Survey Sheet 19.

DISTANCE: 13 miles.

ASCENT: 5,200 ft.

DIFFICULTIES: A fairly serious walk, particularly in winter conditions. It is possible to avoid the main Corrag Bhuidhe traverse by taking a path which avoids the pinnacles, but that takes a lot of interest from the walk. Some Munro-baggers may be happy to take the easy option, though.

ACCOMMODATION: Youth hostels at Ullapool, Aultbea and Carn Dearg, by Gairloch. Hotels, guest-houses and bed-and-breakfast at Dundonnell, Ullapool, Gairloch and Inverewe. Bunk-house at Sail Mhor, Dundonnell.

Between the long arms of Loch Maree and Little Loch Broom, in Wester Ross, lies a great tangle of wild mountain and high, lonely lochans. These days the word 'wilderness' is greatly over-used, and often misapplied, but for the vast deer-forests of Strathnashealag, Fisherfield and Letterewe, 'wilderness' is an apt description.

In the north of this grand area, standing guard over the path that runs south, is the impressive sandstone wedge of An Teallach, The Forge. With its castellated towers, spires and magnificent Coire Toll an Lochain, this mountain has all the attributes of the best mountain in Scotland. It's certainly one of my favourites, and it comes top of the list of many walkers of my aquaintance. But it was not always so. During Thomas Pennant's 'tour' of 1772, he wrote: 'West, a view where the

awful, or rather the horrible, predominates – peaks with sides dark, deep and precipitous; with snowy glaciers lodged in the shaded apertures . . .' How attitudes change!

The best-known view of An Teallach is probably that from the Dundonnell-Braemore road, the old 'Destitution Road'. Three great and imposing ridges, Glas Mheall Mor, Glas Mheall Liath and Sail Liath, separate two impressive corries, Glas Tholl and Toll an Lochain. The main summit, Bidean a'Ghlas Thuill, Peak of the Green, or Grey, Hollow, 3,484 ft, lies at the top of the middle ridge, while a subsidiary summit, another Munro, is Sgurr Fiona, Peak of Wine, 3,474 ft. This top is situated on the very crest of a tight, airy and pinnacled arête which bends round to form the southern ridge, which ends at Sail Liath. This arête crosses four high rock towers, the Corrage Bhuidhe Buttresses, and a tall, overhanging spire which goes by the name of Lord Berkeley's Seat. The traverse demands some fairly exposed scrambling, but a path below the ridge, on the south-west, avoids the difficulties.

The route begins at the Corrie Hallie car-park which is on the A832 road. From here take a track that runs south-west through the trees of Gleann Chaorachain. After half-a-mile or so, cross the Allt Gleann Chaorachain and climb westwards on rocky slabs and heather to reach an obvious quartzite escarpment. Follow this rocky highway to the foot of the Sail Liath ridge.

This is where the hard work starts. Ascend the

broken slabs, grass and scree to the summit of Sail Liath, and cross a col and small peak before dropping to the Cadha Gobhlach, a high, rocky place of immense grandeur. Now for the real excitement. In front and above you rises the steep bulk of the Corrag Bhuidhe Buttresses. A huge, terraced buttress seems to bar the way, but the route is clear enough: just look for the scratch-marks and the worn hand and foot-holds. It's a good scramble, with one awkward slab high up. The crest of the ridge is superb, high and exposed above the black waters of Loch Toll an Lochain, more than 1,000 ft below you. I have mentioned the path running around the south-west side of the ridge, but try not to be tempted by it. The exhilaration of this high route is what this hill is all about.

As you come off Corrag Bhuidhe, so the next obstacle presents itself: Lord Berkeley's Seat. Tip-toe your way up its sandstone steps and look over the summit to the void below. It's impressive. The ridge ends with the first Munro of the day, the shapely peak of Sgurr Fiona.

The going becomes quite steep again after Fiona, as you descend north-north-east over some pretty rocky ground to the obvious col. But there are now no real obstacles, and soon the last good climb of the day presents itself – the long pull on to Bidean a'Ghlas Thuill, 3,484 ft, the summit of An Teallach. To return to Corrie Hallie, descend northwards from the summit to the obvious col and then drop down steep slopes eastwards into Coire a'Ghlas Thuill, taking great care if the ground is snow-covered. Follow the north side of the stream to the Garbh Allt waterfalls, from where a good path takes you back to the A832 road just north of the car-park.

PEERING THROUGH the mist to the gaunt outline of Lord Berkeley's Seat, An Teallach. An easy scramble takes you to the top but beware when you gaze down the other side. There is nothing for some two thousand feet.

Beinn Dearg

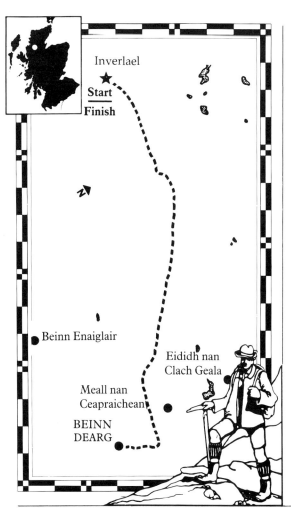

MAP: Ordnance Survey Sheet 20.

DISTANCE: Seven miles.

ASCENT: 3,200 ft.

DIFFICULTIES: A straightforward hill walk with very few problems.

ACCOMMODATION: Hotels, guest-houses and bed-and-breakfast in Ullapool. Youth hostel and camp-sites in Ullapool. Bunk-house at Dundonnell.

Scotland has many Beinn Deargs. The Red Hill is a common-enough description, especially for any north-west facing hill which catches the last light of the dying sun. But Beinn Dearg above Inverlael Forest, just north of the Dirrie More above Ullapool, is special. This is the Beinn Dearg that looks to the sea, as Hamish Brown once described it.

You'll see the massive bulk of this fine hill as you drive over the A835 Ullapool road from Garve. It rears a lofty head beyond the foot of Loch Glascarnoch, beside its near-neighbour, Cona'Mheall, the Enchanted Hill. You can climb these two hills from this approach, and perhaps also take in an ascent of Am Faochagach, which lies slightly to the east. But beware. If you do head in from this direction, choose a day of hard frost, hard enough to freeze the ground, and the bogs, and the oozing peat. This is very wet country, and I've had more saturated feet hereabouts than probably anywhere else in Scotland.

But I believe a better route – and certainly an easier route – is from further down the A835 road, at the head of Loch Broom, a few hundred metres north of Inverlael House. On the north side of the road a private forestry track runs up through the Lael Forest into the lower part of Gleann na Squaib.

This is a much more comfortable approach, a gentler and more gradual climb up a good stalkers' path. Gleann na Squaib is pleasant, with some spectacular waterfalls and good pools for bathing when the weather is warm enough. Higher up the glen, the stalkers' path begins to zig-zag up the steeper inclines, a superbly engineered path which offers some spectacular views of mighty crags formed by the long, sloping shoulder of Beinn Dearg and Diollaid a'Mhill Bhric. These crags are split by half-a-dozen great gullies, most of them good winter-climbs when they're thick with snow.

A STONY PLACE

The cliff line ends in an imposing corner line, a magnificent steep tower which boasts a fairly classic rock-climb called The Tower of Babel, first climbed by the late Dr Tom Patey, Ullapool's doctor, in 1962.

The path soon takes you on to a high and broad pass, a stony place with scattered lochans. To climb Beinn Dearg, which is on your right, follow the line of a massive dry-stane dyke, which

runs up the shoulder of the hill virtually all the way to the summit. Near the top, where the dyke bears west, is a gap in the wall. Go through there, and follow a south-south-west bearing for about 300 metres, and you'll cross the bald dome of the summit slopes and find the 3,547 ft summit itself.

Back at the stony *bealach*, you have a choice of route. You can either continue eastwards to climb Cona' Mheall as well, or continue north to take in two more Munros, Eididh nan Clach Geala, 3,039 ft, and Meall nan Ceapraichean, 3,063 ft. The circut of all four tops makes a very worthwhile day.

These hills have a splendid wilderness quality. Although fairly close to the Ullapool road, they give a feeling of remoteness, created probably by the knowledge that to the north and north-east lie great chunks of wild country, roadless and without habitation. Another Munro, Seana Bhraigh, lies in isolated splendour in the midst of this wilderness. One of the remotest of the Munros, its ascent demands a considerable expedition. It is probably easier climbed from Oykel Bridge, in the north-east.

TIME TO sit and reflect on the wonders of nature, in clear air, while an early morning mist shrouds the land below.

THE IMPRESSIVE skyline of the Coigach peaks stand out against a clear sky. The dominant buttress of Sgurr on Fhidleir juts out in the centre of the picture. A Very Severe rock climb takes the prominent 'nose' of the Fhidleir.

Ben More Coigach and The Fiddler

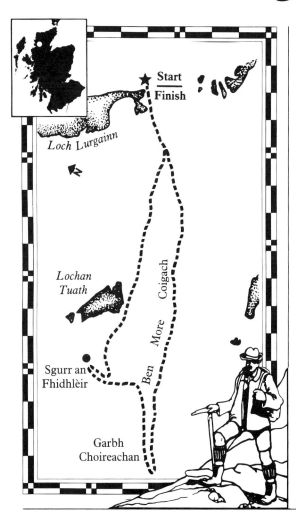

MAP: Ordnance Survey Shet 15.

DISTANCE: 10 miles.

ASCENT: 3,200 ft.

DIFFICULTIES: A generally easy high-level walk in stunning surroundings. The heather-filled gully beside The Fiddler could be difficult in winter under snow. It looks like a certain potential avalanche trap.

ACCOMMODATION: Youth hostel at Ullapool. Camp-sites at Ullapool and Ardmair. Hotels, guest-houses and bed-and-breakfast at Ullapool.

Drive north from Ullapool, up the long, steady incline out of the town, over the high pass, and drop down to Ardmair Bay. There in front of you a spit of white beach curves gracefully out into the sea. The sanctuary of Isle Martin protects it from the gales which whip across the Minch from the Herbrides, and in good weather it's good to wander out along the beach, gazing seawards to where the Summer Isles float on the horizon.

It's a magnificent spot, but the eye is continually led away from the sea to the great wall of weathered sandstone which dominates the northern shore of the bay. It looks precipitous and, more than 1,000 ft high and a mile along. It has an air of barren forboding about it. But continue northwards on the A835 and the character of this mountain mass changes. It soon becomes evident that this long sandstone wall is

but a frontage for a complex system of peaks, glens, ridges, corries and lochans, a relatively unspoiled and even unknown area which compares with some of the better-known classic walking regions of Highland Scotland.

A RARE BLEND

The highest point on the sandstone wall is Ben More Coigach, only 2,438 ft but seeming higher simply because you have to climb it from sea level. The other main peak of the area, Sgurr an Fhidhleir, 2,306 ft, rises to a sharp and dramatic point about a mile along a broad north-west ridge from Ben More. It's a superb high eyrie of a place, with deep, plunging cliffs on three sides and magnificent views of the Summer Isles. In many ways, these hills bring together all the finer characteristics of that rare blend which occurs when mountains and sea come together in dramatic contrast. It's a rare experience you'll find on the Cuillin of Skye and Rhum, and on one or two mainland mountains, Ladhar Beinn, in Knoydart, and Beinn Sgritheall, across Loch Hourn, are two which come to mind.

Turn off the A835 at Drumrunie Junction and follow the minor road for a couple of miles. As everyone else rushes off to climb Stac Pollaidh along the road, park your car and cross the river just east of Loch Lurgainn. Follow the right bank of the Allt Claonaidh as far as Lochan Tuath, which mirrors the mighty north-west prow of Sgurr an Fhidhleir, the Nose of the Fiddler.

Stac Pollaidh

Walkers don't follow the prow. That's the domain of rock-climbers, who are offered a long and serious climb of Very Severe grade, a standard that belies the objective dangers of the route caused by loose rock and vegetated ledges. It was first climbed in 1692.

South of the prow, a prominent heather-filled gully climbs steeply up to the *bealach* between The Fiddler and Ben More Colgach in the south, and from there easy slopes lead to the summit of The Fiddler itself, a stunning place with magnificent views.

Retrace your steps back to the broad *bealach* and climb the easy, grassy slopes to Ben More Coigach itself. The mile-long south-west ridge towards Garbh Choireachan is well worth exploring if you have time. A succession of rocky towers and good, sandy paths make this ridge an absolute delight, with wonderful views out over the Summer Isles and across the Minch to Harris and Lewis. On a good day you'll see the Cuillin of Skye, the Torridon hills. An Teallach, the Beinn Dearg hills and, of course, the mighty hills of the far north.

From the summit of Ben More Coigach, descend to the small *bealach* below Speicin Coinnich, and then down the steep slopes towards Beinn Tarsuinn. Continue over the summit and down steep, heathery slopes back to the Allt Claonaidh and the boggy path back to your car.

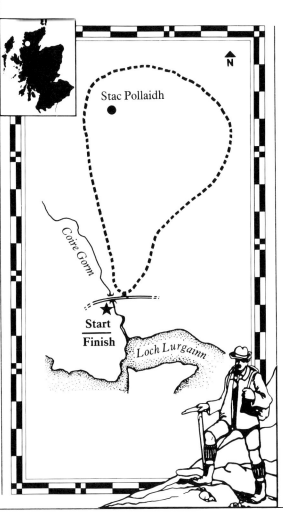

MAP: Ordnance Survey Sheet 15.

DISTANCE: 3½ miles.

ASCENT: 1,900 ft.

DIFFICULTIES: To reach the summit demands some scrambling over large, exposed sandstone blocks. Otherwise, a short easy mountain walk.

ACCOMMODATION: Youth hostel in Ullapool. Camp-sites in Ullapool, Ardmair and Achiltibuie. Hotels, guest-houses and bed-and-breakfast in Ullapool.

Stac Pollaidh, on the edge of Sutherland, has been described as the 'perfect miniature'. It's also been described as impudent and preposterous, and yet again likened to a 'fossilised stegosaurus'. It's all of these, and is most certainly unique.

Drive over the road north from Ullapool and see it appear beyond the tree-lined lochan at Drumrunie. On first viewing, it makes you gasp. It's so other-worldly. Its impudence makes you smile inwardly. Rising from the surrounding moorland, it thrusts its jagged crest into the sky with bravado, small but cock-sure, dominating in its miniature scale. Within a Cuillin range, or a Torridon range, it would lose some of its character, but rising from the Sutherland moors, separated from its neighbours by a lot of space, its individuality reigns supreme.

The base rock of the area tends to be grey Lewisian gneiss, formed 1,500 million years ago.

LOOKING NORTH from Stac Pollaidh to Cul Mor. The north west ridge of Cul Beag is just visible on the right. Much of this land belongs to the Inverpolly National Nature Reserve and is looked after by the Nature Conservancy Council.

But again Stac Pollaidh shows her individuality. She is made of red sandstone, laid down on top of the gneiss about 800 million years ago. The grinding Ice Ages, and subsequent weathering of frost and coarse winds from the Minch, have worn down this sandstone into the ragged, spiky crest that is so familiar today.

CRUEL GUARDIANS

I've visited Stac Pollaidh many times over the years, but my last visit was a day of days. We camped in Ullapool and I slept outside, below a velvety sky that turned light just after two o'clock. By seven the sun was hot, too hot to lie in a sleeping bag. It was a perfect day for the perfection of that Sutherland landscape.

Stac Pollaidh rises on its south side, its Loch Lurgainn side, in three great steps. As you climb the hill, so the angle continues to steepen until you have to scramble the last few hundred feet. It was too hot for that sort of sweaty attack, so we took a footpath around the eastern slopes of the hill, gradually winding our way upwards in a manner which exposed new and superlative views with each step. First of all, Cul Beag, a massive triangular wedge, lording it above the eastern edges of Loch Lurgainn. Then, as we circumavigated the hill, Cul Mor came into view, a bigger, more complicated topography, dominating the magnificent hinterland of the Inverpolly National Nature Reserve, a loch-studded paradise. Here and there, fringes of bright-green birch hung on to craggy ravines, luscious dots of vegetation in a landscape otherwise virtually desert.

As we approached the northern slopes of Pollaidh, her northern neighbour, Suilven, came in sight. What another majestic hill this is, the Sugarloaf mountain of Sutherland. I remembered another stifling hot day a few years ago when we traversed Suilven from Elphin. We couldn't stop for long because of the voraciousness of the clegs, and we leapt like madmen into lochans at every opportunity. We were in our tent at seven o'clock that night, bruised and bitten and under remorseless attack from midges. These are the true guardians of these wild areas . . . May the Lord protect them!

Soon we stood on the high *bealach* that is the summit of Stac Pollaidh to so many people. To stand on the true summit demands some commitment, for it is an exposed and rocky scramble which calls for some skill in route-finding, too. But most are happy enough to sit among the rocky pinnacles of this narrow saddle, to eat their lunch and soak up the views towards Coigach, and westwards to the Hebrides.

Suilven

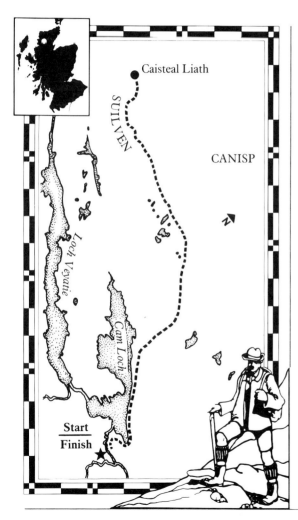

MAP: Ordnance Survey Sheet 15.

DISTANCE: Through-route, 16 miles.

ASCENT: 3,000 ft.

DIFFICULTIES: A long, rough walk, but no real problems. The only straightfoward means of ascent are either the north or the south approach to the Bealach Mor. The ascent of either of the tops by other routes involves climbing.

ACCOMMODATION: Hotels, guest-houses, bed-and-breakfast in Lochinver and Ullapool.

Now and again, but probably more again than now, I find myself questioning the whole business of hill-wandering. At certain times of the year in particular, when usually it's so difficult to tell what the weather is going to do, I have an inborn reluctance to plan days out. If the weather's reasonable, I go; if it's not, I don't. But when all the delights of the outdoors disease clash together in a great unplanned mêlée of delight and joy, then the question 'Why?' seems irrelevant.

I had a night in Sutherland recently just like that. Just to be there was a delight in itself, as it always is, but on this day, Sutherland was wearing its wilderness gown with all the subtletly and poise of a model. It was beautiful, yet mysterious and provocative; gloriously brash in a riot of sunset colour, but at the same time as delicate as pastels.

I camped at a favourite site, a lochside glory-

hole of real charm near Suilven. As so many times before, I didn't see another soul for a couple of days. The silence deafened, a sensation which is as pure and clean as the crystal-cold water which pours off the hillside into the loch. I had walked into this place of places from Elphin on the A835 Ullapool-Assynt road, a walk that was just long enough to let the mind sort out the myriad of thoughts that pulse through the brain when you start a trip like this.

Gradually, with the miles, the thoughts straighten out; the unimportant is cast aside, and the flow settles down to what is important: the shape of that distant hill, the stag on the far horizon, the spiralling buzzard in the sky. Shackles of civilisation are cast aside and the simple chores of campcraft become automatic. Collect some water, pump-up the petrol stove, get the food in the pot, and eat it. A dram and cigar follow (two shackles of civilisation which are quite harmonious in the wilds), and an early night under the stars.

GLASSY WATERS

I was up early in the morning, before it was light. A frost shimmered on the dry ground and my breath hung in curtains before me, even in the tent. Pricked and hurried by the cold, I made breakfast, opened the flap of the tent from the warmth of my sleeping-bag, and took in the scene before me. Immediately in front, the waters of Lochan Fhada were like glass. Across the loch, the tangle of heather and scree gave way to the rising flanks of Canisp, a fine-enough mountain in its own right, but much dominated in these surroundings by the Matterhorn shape of Suilven, the uncontested showpiece of Sutherland.

Readers who know Suilven may be surprised by my description of it as a spire. From Stac Pollaidh or Cul Mor in the south, its shape is more that of a stretched-out sugarloaf, but from where I lay, looking at it from virtually due east, it appeared as a great black monolith, rising from its bedrock plinth of Lewissian gneiss. As I gazed at it, so it began to change colour, from black to orange, then to pastel pink and blue as the rising wintry sun slowly gave it life.

WARM MEMORIES

Hours later I stood on its summit, having climbed it by the only real breach in its defences, up steep slopes to the Bealach Mor, the mountain's natural waistline. I gazed across the sea to the hills of Harris. Behind me, my campsite of the night before had completely lost its identity, swallowed up in an anonymity of rolling lochan-splattered moorland. To the south, the tops of Cul Mor and Cul Beag beckoned, and the backside of Stac Pollaidh showed its more private face.

Memories flooded back of a trip years ago across this wild moorland in a heatwave, when clegs and midges had attacked us at every opportunity. How different to to-day, with the winter cold nipping harshly at exposed skin. It was not a day to linger on the tops. A car was waiting for me at Lochinver, but not before some more shackles of civilisation, a pie and a pint in the pub.

LOOKING ACROSS the Inverpolly Nature Reserve to Suilven. This is a remote wild area of flat moorland, scatterd lochans and strange brooding mountains like Suilven.

Suilven can equally well be climbed in a day, either from Lochinver and back, a 13-mile walk with about 3,000 ft of ascent, or by the route I have described, as a through-route from Elphin to Lochinver. If you can arrange the transport, try the latter; there's something particularly satisfying about a journey of this type.

6. Badenoch

Drumochter, so often gloomy, a dirge after the green lushness of Atholl, can pull off surprises that leave you breathless.

Drive over the new A9 on an autumn evening, as the sun drops low, casting long shadows over that high, lumpy hill, the Boar of Badenoch, and you won't see a beauty to match, say, Slioch across Loch Maree, or the Pass of Glen Coe, but what you will experience is an atmosphere caused by the interspersing of light and shadow, colour and shape, rounded, smooth and gentle, and wholly Badenoch. It's a far-flung, forest-girdled place, sweeping away on long mountain slopes on either side of the River Spey.

It's hard to find the words to describe it. No doubt the Gaelic, that beautifully descriptive language, has a word for it. Anglo-Saxon seems to be devoid of words that singularly reflect beauty. Were our southern ancestors so lacking in appreciation, or sensitivity? Were they blind to this kind of beauty, or was it just outwith their ken?

I suspect it's a combination of several things. The Gaels were, and still are, sensitive and emotional. In a sense they were earth-tied. Theirs was a living landscape, a part of their whole being, an integral part of their very existence, their life-pulse.

Sadly, we've largely lost that bond, and perhaps that's why our acceptance of such beauty is so limp. Others see the earth and its living things in a supernatural light, and believe that this whole living, pulsing, vibrant creation should be worshipped as a god, a god of harvest, a god of giving. Many of them claim the title of New Age, but their thoughts are ancient, as old as the Druids and the idol-worshippers and the pagans. Nothing's new.

SOFT VEILS

But it's easy to become caught up in fanciful theologies when faced with the single-malt variety of beauty that Badenoch offers. It's untarnished, this combination of hill and glen, light and shadow, sun and cloud, often softened by the delicate subtlety of a smir of rain, a soft veil cast over the hardness of rock and scraggy heather. Here, too, is a corner of Scotland steeped in history and tradition, a land of legend and song, from the controversial lore of Ossianic claims, through the ancient tales of Fingalian legend, to the inevitable wanderings of Prince Charles Edward Stuart and his followers.

Basically, to those who live here, Badenoch is another world, sequestered from the south by the high miles of Drumochter Pass. This is the very heartland of the Central Highlands. Its western border is the historic Druim Alban, the backbone of Scotland; the high Monadhliath mountains guard it on the north and the high tops of the Cairngorms and their western spurs rise to the south; and through the broad valley between flows the longest river in Scotland, the Spey.

An old description of the Spey, dating from the seventeenth century, claims:

Of tymes this river in tymes of speat or stormie weather will be alse bigg as if it were a Logh, and also als broad and overflowes all the low corne lands of the Countrey next to itself.

Indeed, the very title of Badenoch, or Baideanach, the submerged or drowned land, neatly reflects the quirkiness of this river. In times of heavy rain, which is less common in Badenoch than in other areas, the Spey has an urge to become a series of lochs, particularly in the low haughs between Kingussie and Kincraig, where it swells and takes over the adjacent water-meadows and rough grazings until the great fen area beyond Ruthven Barracks becomes a sea of unbroken waters.

RIVER CONTRASTS

When you consider that the Spey drains an area of some 1,300 square miles of mountainous terrain, and has a flow of 98 miles, with numerous tributaries, then it's hardly surprising that its largely narrows banks will fail to contain it once in a while, expecially when the spring winds breathe and begin to melt the mountain snows.

The Spey is a river of contrasts. Rising high in the emptiness of the Monadhliath Mountains, it has something less of a tempestous youth than its near-neighbour, the Dee, which falls from more than 4,000 ft to less than 2,000 ft in only a few

APPROACHING THE Bealach Dubh, with Ben Alder under winter cloud on the left. Ben Alder is one of the most remote mountains in the country and a winter expedition is a serious undertaking.

REINDEER ON the Cairngorm plateau. Reindeer became extinct in Scotland hundreds of years ago but were re-introduced in the nineteen fifties. They are now farmed by the Cairngorm Reindeer Company and are a common sight on the Cairngorm Plateau.

THE CRAGS of Creag Meagaidh. In winter these vegetated cliffs often become encased in snow and ice and then offer tremendous sport to winter climbers.

short miles. The Spey matures rapidly, pouring below the old Wade Bridge at Garvamore, beyond Laggan, but soon begins to quieten considerably, and by the time it's passed Newtonmore and Kingussie, it has become a meandering river of some grace, not entirely sluggish, but stately with maturity.

ANCIENT RELICS

Badenoch, unlike many areas in the Highlands, is well wooded. Native birch abounds, and here and there ancient relics of the great Pine Forest of Caledon still survive. What happened to that truly enormous forest? We can look back 3,000 or 4,000 years to the era of the Picts, or the proto-Picts, a polyandrous, matriarchal series of societies constantly preoccupied with looking for or creating clearings among the fearful forests that harboured wolves and bears. The young sons were obliged to move further and further away from their parents' holdings, to shielings that were progressively enlarged by the use of the axe and fire. The Roman influence on the Highlands can largely be ignored, but not that of the ruthless Norsemen, who burned and pillaged their way into the interior.

The process has been repeated over the centuries, and reached a climax with the terrible evictions in the early part of the nineteenth century, when, to make grazing grounds for sheep, countless thousands of Scots pine were incinerated by the fire-sticks of the flockmasters.

But compared to other areas of the Highlands, Badenoch got off lightly. Local tradition explains it in a more colourful, if less factual, way. King of Lochlann, being envious of the fine forests of the Scottish Highlands, sent a witch across the waters from Norway. This ancient hag had a simple duty to perform: Starting in the north, she would supernaturally reign down fire from the skies.

She remained invisible as she carried out these fearful deeds by hiding behind the clouds, and her devastation left the Highlands as a smouldering morass. But as her red-hot fires reached the northern edge of the Badenoch district, a man of the area hit upon a plan to make the witch reveal herself.

He gathered together a huge number of cattle, sheep and horses; then separated the cows from their calves, the sheep from their lambs, the foals from the mares. The outcry from the young beasts was so loud and pitiful that the witch, in alarm and astonishment, stuck her head out of the cloud behind which she was hiding. The wise man of Badenoch, having taken the precaution of loading his gun with a silver sixpence, made no mistake in his aim and brought the Norwegian witch tumbling down to earth.

And so some of Badenoch's glory was saved. How much less the view down Loch Laggan from Gergask would be without the wooded shores of Ardverikie. The great crag of Creag Dubh at Newtonmore would appear naked without her flanks of russet birch woods, and the steep, rounded profile of the Glen Feshie hills, those outliers of the high Sgurans, would lack their chief claim to fame, that of Scotland's highest-growing native Caledonian pines, where these gnarled old 'redskins' grow at a height of 2,000 ft.

And how the wildlife would have suffered. As we lost the wild boar and the bear, the wolf and beaver from the early pine forests, so we would have lost the capercaille and the crested tit, the

THE SKI grounds in Coire Cas of Cairngorm. The ski-ing here is arguably the best in Scotland with the best conditions normally found between February and April. There is much opposition though to any further westwards extension to these ski grounds.

pine marten and the red quirrel, the crossbill and siskin, creatures of the pine woods all.

But visitors to Badenoch can still see some of these native Highland species which are now otherwise extinct within these shores. The Highland Wildlife Park at Kincraig exhibits only species which are, or were at one time, indigenous to Scotland. Visitors are often surprised to find bison roaming the policies, and wolves, beavers, lynx and bears within their various enclosures.

The settlements of man have quite naturally developed on the broad valley floor, where the mountain valleys extend down to the plain and where the river systems meet. Kingussie and Newtonmore are both sizeable villages, tussling for the accolade of Scotland's shinty capital and where that rough-and-tumble sport 'enjoys' the partisanship and passion of an Old Firm rivalry. Laggan and Dalwhinnie are smaller, more remotely independent, while Kincraig, closer to the affluence of the tourist shrine at Aviemore, enjoys the quiet conservatism of a place to which owners of holiday homes retire.

SNOW STARVATION

All, to a greater or lesser degree, bow to tourism. The ski-development on Cairngorm extends its influence far and wide, its long tentacles probing deep into Badenoch. Here the hotels and guest-houses are promised a winter trade, provided Biera, Queen of the Winter Snows, remembers. In recent years, snow starvation has been acute, affecting jobs and security, but, in a more positive sense, making tourist operators realise that Badenoch and neighbouring Strathspey have more to offer during winter than just ski-ing.

Forest walks abound, and the flatness of the strath is ideal for cycling. More estates are offering farm tours, and the ever-popular Highland Folk Museum in Kingussie has spawned a brand new Highland Folk Park just down the road at Newtonmore. The visitor to Badenoch rarely lacks things to do, at any time of the year.

In between the villages, the land is farmed and forested, and the ubiquitious sheep share the lesser ground where the fields give way to the moorlands, which in turn give way to the coarse heather and scree of the high tops.

Colours dominate. To the north and west, the Grey Hills, the Monadhliath, lie as a great clenched fist, the fingers of which run down into bonnie Glen Banchor as great ridges. In between the red deer roam, and above the golden eagle searches for mountain hare. On the other side of the Spey, the mighty Cairngorms, the Blue Hills, take their name from the most obvious hill in the range, Cairngorm of the ski-development, of the Lurcher's Gully controversy, and of the £10 million-a-year turnover in ski-related tourism. And like the ski industry, and the tourism, this name of the mountain range is comparatively new. Until fairly recently, these hills were known as the Monadh Ruadh, the Red Hills, named after the pink, coarse granite which glows rosily in the setting sun. But few nowadays know them as the Monadh Ruadh, and even fewer are those who would recognise that name at all.

While the skiers flock to the packed snow-slopes in winter, and the hill-walkers to the other high tops, so the ornithologists take up summer residence in the pine forests and woodlands. Badenoch's chief ornithological claim to fame is the area known as the Insh Marshes, the flood plains of the Spey between Kingussie and Loch Insh.

This area has been made a reserve by the Royal Society for the Protection of Birds, and from the wooden hides you can look out on to several natural pools, fringed by birch and juniper woodland. These are great places to enjoy the antics of the redshank, whooper swans, snipe, lapwings and curlew. The cacaphony of black-headed gulls, the *Larus ridibundus* are inland-nesters and are almost as common in Badenoch as chaffinches.

BOTANIC INTEREST

The Insh Marshes Reserve is also a good place for botanists. The area is of considerable national interest, with important sedge communities. Aquatic plants, as might be expected in an area which in reality is a northern fenland, are numerous.

Local species include least yellow water-lily and greater bladderwort, and species such as valerian, angelica and cowbane can be found. Closer to the Spey, on the grassy banks that have been built up over the years to try to minimise the flooding, is a wide variety of different plants, including, surprisingly, mountain pansy, melancholy thistle and wood cranesbill.

The habitat in many ways is an unusual one for a Scottish reserve, with a vast area of sedge fen. Found in all the wetter parts of the reserve, it gives way to reeds in the areas of shallow standing water. Drier areas of the reserve have rough pasture, but invading patches of willow carr have formed large areas of scrub, and beside the river are large stands of willow, cherry and alder.

As the flatness of the flood plain eases on to

higher ground, the marshy ground gives way to birch woodland, mixed with its common companion, juniper. All this mixter-maxter of habitat makes for a tremendous variety of bird-life, both resident and migrant.

FEATHERED VARIETY

The reserve is a principal place for wintering whooper swans, having at one time more than one per cent of the north-west European population. Greylag geese are common, too, and most common of the wintering duck are mallard, teal, widgeon, tufted duck and goldeneye. Occasional pairs of shovelers have been seen, and goosanders and red-brested mergansers are present in small numbers. The large fen areas offers a home to birds such as the meadow-pipit, and reed-buntings breed in the damper areas. In the scrub are sedge- and willow-warblers and a few pairs of grasshopper warblers arrive in most years.

Surprisingly to many people, birds of prey are not unknown on Insh Marshes. You may spot an osprey fishing in the Spey, a hen-harrier, buzzards (which are the only breeding bird of prey species on the reserve), sparrowhawks or a peregrine falcon.

But the best time to visit the marshes is in the spring, when the waders are the real performers. Curlews never fail to delight with their drawn-out cries, and the trumpeting of lapwings, or *teuchits*, as they're known locally, seems always so defiant. The oyster-catchers, too, add an urgency to the proceedings, as do the sandpipers; and the full orchestration of sound exudes life and excitement, the expectancy of the new season.

The seasons are important in Badenoch. While for many years nearby Aviemore has proclaimed itself Scotland's all-year-round holiday centre, it's taken a while for the Badenoch villages to jump on the bandwagon. A ski-development proposal in Drumochter Pass has been approved and will possibly be functional in the early '90s, and the hoteliers and guest-house owners of Newtonmore and Laggan see themselves in a nice position once the new Aonach Mor development, near Fort William, gets underway in a couple of years' time. Being virtually halfway between Cairngorm and Aonach Mur, they feel that many skiers will plan their holiday in Badenoch, to take advantage of the best snow conditions east or west.

But ski-developments or not, it's hard to shake the traditions of old Highland villages. All the Badenoch villages lack the brashness and high-octane promotion of Aviemore, and for many people, and for many skiers, too, this is a plus. There is a leaning still towards tradition, and the Highland Folk Museum in Kingussie, and the brand-new Highland Folk Park (due to open in 1990), foster this 'heritage link'. The Laggan Co-operative, a dynamic local group which runs the village hall, the local shop and the petrol station, has plans to turn the old Kingshouse at Garvamore into an interpretative centre for Scotland's Military Roads. The plans include also a hostel for the increasing number of hill-walkers who tramp over General Wade's Corrieyairack Pass from Fort Augustus at the head of Loch Ness.

The very same building was used by Charles Edward Stuart after he had tramped over the Corrieyairack with his Jacobite army. He came to know Badenoch pretty well during that campaign. In a cave on Ben Alder, high above the waters of Loch Ericht, he stayed for a while with one of his supporters, Cluny MacPherson, himself outlawed for his role in the uprising. On another of his long treks, in fact *en route* to Ben Alder, the Prince crossed the shoulder of Creag Meagaidh through a narrow *bealach* called The Window. It was the remnants of the Jacobite army which reputedly burned down the Ruthven Barracks, near Kingussie, in their flight from the savagery of Culloden.

Nowadays, a growing army of hill-walkers and climbers takes to the mountain byeways and hills of Badenoch. The high tops of the Cairngorms exert an Arctic pull on thousands each year, while the delights of the Monadhliath are less obvious, and less publicised. Fewer still are those who tramp the rounded tops of Drumochter, or penetrate into the wilderness of Ardverikie or Pattack, where the hills have a reputation of remoteness. Here the miles are long and often hard, but the reward is a good handful of Munros, those mountains which attain the height of 3,000 ft above sea-level.

Badenoch boasts more than a good share of Munros, and the hill-goer is easily satisfied. So, too, are the sportsmen, the deer-stalkers and the anglers, the grouse-shooters and those who are content to blast away at clay-pigeons. But for all the efforts to mix modern tourism with traditional pastimes, one thing remains constant: the grandeur of the land, the very quality that attracts people time and time again. And that brings me back to where I started, on the high road over Drumochter, wondering what surprise Badenoch is going to pull off this time.

Ben Alder, Badenoch

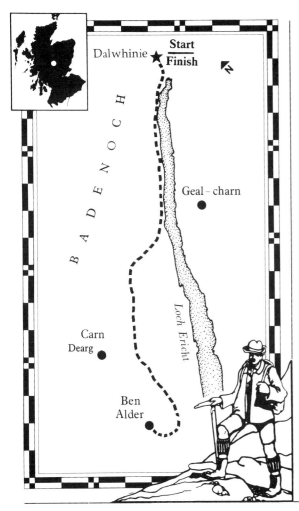

MAP: Ordnance Survey Sheet 42.

DISTANCE: 20 miles.

ASCENT: 3,500 ft.

DIFFICULTY: A long and serious walk, especially in winter when an overnight stop at either Culra Bothy or McCook's Bothy at Ben Alder Bay would be necessary. Navigation can often be difficult on the summit plateau. Permission can be asked to drive to Loch Pattack from Dalwhinnie. Telephone 05282–224 (Ben Alder Estate).

ACCOMMODATION: Youth hostels at Kingussie, Aviemore and Pitlochry. Hotels, guest-houses and bed-and-breakfast at Dalwhinnie, Laggan, Newtonmore and Kingussie.

Often, as I have driven south on the A9 near Dalwhinnie, my eye has been led down the great geological fault that holds Loch Ericht to the vast buttressed form of Ben Alder. In winter garb, the mountain appears closer than its 12 or so miles, often fooling visitors into believing that they can 'knock it off' fairly quickly. Not so. This hill stands proud and aloof, distant in terms of mileage and remoteness, and it's all the better for that.

Ben Alder is a vast, high plateau, containing about 400 acres of ground higher than 3,500 ft. Cairngorm-like, it is surrounded by fine corries, particularly those facing east, the Gabhacorries. These fall into the high-level Loch a'Bhealaich Bheithe, beyond which lies, like a cradling arm, the ridge of Beinn Bheoil, at 3,333 ft, another Munro.

A good Land-Rover track borders the northern shores of Loch Ericht, starting of just beyond the railway station in Dalwhinnie. It is possible to get permission from the estate to drive a car six or seven miles down the track to Pattack, but the local keeper, Geordie Oswald, claims that his white garrons, the horses used for deer-stalking, are partial to eating wing-mirrors and have a fascination for parked cars. Risk it at will.

I've often walked down this track, impatient to reach the remote delights of Loch Pattack and Ben Alder, but nevertheless enjoying the bright-yellow broom and the bleached stumps of ancient pines which line the loch. But I've often cursed the monotony of this track when returning home in the opposite direction. How great is the motivation of anticipation. What's the occasional wing-mirror, anyway?

Soon the heart quickens as the track swings west, past the old grey lodge and on to the flats of Pattack. Beyond, the gaping jaws of the Bealach Dubh, the Black Pass between Ben Alder and the Lancet Edge, draws you onwards. But that's not your route today. Instead, follow the Allt a'Chaoil-reidhe, the river that runs down from the Bealach Dubh, and soon, after passing the squat building that is Culra Bothy, you meet another stream, running into the Allt 'Chaoil-reidhe from Loch a' Bhealaich Bheithe above.

BEN ALDER.
Permission is often given by the keeper at Ben Alder Lodge to take your car up from Dalwhinnie to Loch Pattack. What the keeper doesn't tell you is that his white garrons have a habit of chewing your wing mirrors. Probably better to walk in all the way.

Follow the burn up to the loch, and then take the steep slopes on your left to the summit ridge of Beiunn Bheoil, a well-positioned top, high above the long, sinuous Loch Ericht stretching south to the edges of Rannoch Moor. Continue south to the top of Sron Coire na h-Iolaire and enjoy the view down to Ben Alder Bay with its a good bothy (McCook's Bothy). Descend to the Bealach Breabag, and then climb steep, bouldery ground north-westwards to reach the extensive summit plateau of Ben Alder itself. A turn to the north beyond a small hump leads to a shallow depression cutting across the route to the summit. A triangulation pillar lords it over the surrounding view, with a smaller cairn beside it.

Rather than return by the same route, cross the stony plateau north-eastwards to where two prominent ridges lead down into the glen. The southern ridge is called the Short Leachas, the northern one the Long Leachas. I recommend the latter for its better position and superior views. Take care on the ridge, for it's rocky here and there, but shouldn't present any real difficulties. Return to the track by the Allt a'Chaoil-reidhe, back over Pattack, and to Dalwhinnie by the Loch Ericht track. This is when you wish you'd brought a bicycle.

ALDER BAY, Ben Alder Cottage, the Bealach Breabag and the bulk of Ben Alder itself. Legend has it that Cluny MacPherson, chief of the Clan MacPherson and a lieutenant of Prince Charles Edward Stuart hid in a cave high above the bay after the rout at Cullodon in 1746.

Creag Meagaidh, Badenoch

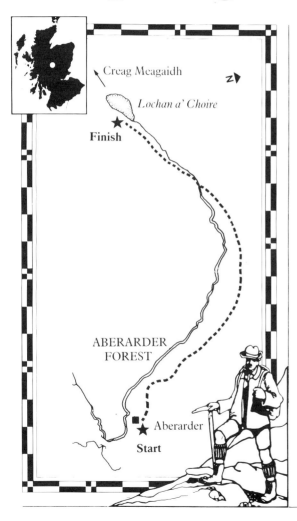

MAP: Ordnance Survey Sheet 34.

DISTANCE: Low-level, seven miles. High-level, 16 miles.

ASCENT: 4,500 ft.

DIFFICULTIES: Easy and straightfoward low-level walk. The high-level alternative is a serious walk, and care should be taken with navigation in bad weather.

ACCOMMODATION: Hotels, guest-houses and bed-and-breakfast at Laggan, Spean bridge, Roybridge, Newtonmore and Kingussie. Youth hostel at Kingussie. Camp-sites at Newtonmore and Roybridge.

Lying just north of the A86 Spean Bridge to Laggan road, the great whale-backed massif of Creag Meagaidh has been a popular area for climbers and walkers for generations.

She's a contrary mountain in many ways. Straddling the historic Druim Alba, the backbone and watershed of Scotland, she can offer delights when other areas are bad, and, conversely, she can hold a miserable huddle of cloud when elsewhere is clear. But when Creag Meagaidh smiles, she grins a great toothless welcome which shows off her vast cavernous Coire Ardair to the best possible advantage.

It's this great array of sheer cliffs which makes Creag Meagaidh so special, held tightly in the vice-like corrie, the cliffs run for more than a mile, and in places rise higher than 1,500 ft (450 m) above the waters of Lochan a' Choire. Indeed,

Coire Ardair is breached only by the long, winding glen which approaches the cliffs and a high 'window', a high-level pass created by glaciation, and much more recently used by the Royal gangrel, Charles Edward Stuart, Bonnie Prince Charlie, on his post-Culloden epic from Cameron country to the hospitality offered by his Jacobite compatriot Cluny MacPherson in Badenoch.

LOW LEVEL CHOICES

The mountaineer's interest in Coire Ardair lies on the cliffs when they become plastered with snow and ice in winter. In summer, the rock is too loose and friable for good rock-climbing. For mountain-walkers, the round of Carn Liath, Poite Coire Ardair, Creag Meagaidh and Beinn a Chaorainn makes a marvellous walk of some 16 miles (26 k), offering four Munros, (mountains higher than 3,000 ft) and a day of fine high-level walking.

A pleasant low-level walk runs for $3\frac{1}{2}$ miles (6 k) from Aberarder Farm on Loch Lagganside to the head of the corrie by Lochan a'Choire, and the same distance back down again. All of the walk is on a footpath, and all you'll need is a set of waterproofs and a pair of good stout trainers or walking-boots, a good low-level alternative when the weather is bad on the high tops.

Aberarder Farm is a few miles west of Kinlochlaggan on the A86. Large signs indicate that you're about to enter the Creag Meagaidh

CREAG MEAGAIDH is a massive hill which lies on the very backbone of Scotland, the Druim Alba. As such the weather can often be good here when it is bad on Ben Nevis and likewise it can often be fair here when the clouds are down on Cairngorm in the east.

National Nature Reserve, and you can park your car at the entrance to the Reserve.

Behind the old farm buildings and the new interpretative centre, a good track crosses the lower moorland and for a while runs close to the waters of the Allt Coire Ardair. This track wends its way slowly north and west into the very heart of Coire Ardair, with high hills on either side and the prospect of the Creag Meagaidh cliffs constantly opening up in front of you. Look out for golden eagle spiralling slowly in the thermals high above the glen.

Leave the farm by the gate and take the footpath over the flat, often boggy, moorland. It soon begins to climb gently, and you'll appreciate the work the Nature Conservancy Council has done in its footpath maintenance and restoration. Old railway sleepers take on a new lease of life, but not in the industrial aspect of their former use. A rough bitumen disguises them and offers good traction for slippery boots, while the remorseless grasses and heathers have quickly claimed the sleepers as their own. In a couple of years, you'll never know they are there.

FORESTRY CONTROVERSY

As you wander along the track, your eye will undoubtedly be caught by the high expanse of heather-covered hillside above. Hill-walkers will leave the track and climb their way to the stony top of Carn Liath, the Grey Cairn, and perhaps even follow the high-level traverse to Poite Coire Ardair and Creag Meagaidh itself. Watch out for herds of deer on the steep slopes, or blue hares which turn white in winter as camouflage against the snows.

Across the river to your left stands a fine natural birch-wood, a clump of trees which created some controversy a few years ago.

In 1986, the Creag Meagaidh Estate and Aberarder Farm were bought by the Nature Conservancy Council. Before this a private forestry company had announced plans that would have meant a mass-afforestation of the lower slopes of the mountain, which would possibly have endangered the extensive natural birch-wood which carpets much of lower Coire Ardair. The NCC was keen to protect those woods and, of course, the associated wildlife as well as giving a measure of protection to the birds of the higher hills, birds such as the ptarmigan, dotterel and golden eagle.

AUTUMN GLORY

If you can, plan this walk in the autumn, when the colours are at their finest. The birches will be at their fiery best, and you will walk to the accompaniment of the roar of rutting stags. From all sides these great belly-roars will raise their challenge, a primeval sound full of the spirit of these wild places. During September and October the stags will protect and mate with their harem of hinds, holding off the challenge from younger stags eager to take over the herd. It's a hard time for the red deer, and it's small wonder that once the mating season is over, the stags wander off together and pay little attention to the hinds until the next rut: a stag party in reverse.

The hillside becomes more rugged and steep as you progress. You become aware of entering the sanctuary of the upper corrie. On quiet days it's like entering a hushed cathedral, with awesome rocky crags in front of you, fringed well into the summer with white snow cornices. It's a good place to be, with the cliffs reflected from the still waters of the loch. Ravens grunt their way among the high buttresses, and around you wheatears sing cockily from the top of the rocks. Wander around the shores of the loch before returning back down the path, towards Aberarder Farm.

A'Chailleach, Badenoch

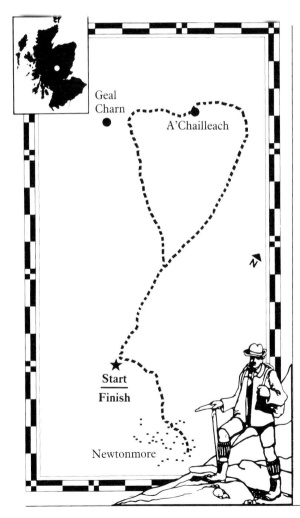

MAP: Ordnance Survey Sheet 35.

DISTANCE: 12 miles.

ASCENT: 2,200 ft.

DIFFICULTIES: A straightfoward walk. The only difficulties could be on the ascent of the ridge to the summit plateau. Take care in snow conditions. Makes an ideal half-day walk in summer.

ACCOMMODATION: Youth hostel at Kingussie. Hotels, guest-houses and bed-and-breakfast in Newtonmore, Laggan and Kingussie.

Blizzards and 60-mile-an-hour winds had been forecast, with temperatures on the summits as low as minus seven degrees.

Only the night before I had travelled north through Drumochter Pass, a nightmare drive into almost horizontal snow flakes. At times I couldn't see the line of the road, despite dropping my speed right down. As I drove off the A9 into Newtonmore, I almost skidded into a field. The surface of the road was like a skating rink.

Next morning dawned white, with a fresh covering of snow muffling sound and muting the steams and burns.

Desperately in need of exercise, I took my skis and went to the golf-course, but that wasn't too clever. The snow was soft and fresh, and the ground below wet and warm, after weeks of unseasonal mildness. My friend, John, had great difficulty in making his waxless skis glide. They kept balling up with the fresh, wet snow, one of the big problems with this kind of ski. I could sense his frustration, and the hills north of the village looked inviting. We swopped ski-boots for walking-boots, picked up a couple of ice-axes and a piece, and settled on a stravaig towards A'Chailleach, Newtonmore's local Munro. It was an inspired choice.

The blizzards and storms forecast for the Cairngorms didn't materialise. Instead, we were treated to an afternoon of bright sunshine, with some sweeping snow-flurries which merely veiled the brightness of the sun from time to time. We took the Glen Road, which runs up into Glen Banchor from Newtonmore's Main Street, and followed the course of the Allt a'Chaorainn high into its corrie to settle for a good snow-and-heather scramble of the hills' north-east-facing slopes.

Allt a'Chaorainn runs down from Coire a'Chaorainn and into the River Calder in Glen Banchor. A motorable road runs up the glen to the Shepherd's Bridge, where there is some car-parking space. A good footpath runs northwards beside a forestry plantation, through a gate and along the western lower slopes of Creag an Loin. The track soon turns into a narrow trace of a path, which drops down beside the Allt a'Chaorainn.

A'Chailleach is often regarded as a dull hill, but it offers its best profile from this unusual angle. The north-east-facing corrie, which is the hill's most redeeming feature, is hardly spectacular, but on a day such as this, with snow swathing the steep, rocky flanks of its north-east buttress, there's fun, and not a little challenge, to be had following the line of least resistance up through the rock-bands and steep terraces.

The snow was still soft, but in the higher reaches the ground below was firm enough to take a well-aimed ice-axe. This allowed us to tackle slightly steeper ground than normal, and it was fun weaving through and over the rock buttresses, wondering what the next stretch would hold.

In summer conditions, this ridge offers an interesting scramble, but it's not difficult and is without doubt the most sporting way to the top. There's also a grand feeling of remoteness, high in this corner of the Monadhliath Hills. These 'Grey Hills' have often been accused of being dull, but I have never found them so. Sure, they have no grand pinnacles or spires or rocky peaks, but there is an open-wide aspect to these hills, a feeling of vast skyscapes and spaciousness, and you'll see more wildlife in them in a day than you would in the Skye Cuillin in a week.

RELATIVE SHELTER

All too soon our scramble was over, and we topped out on hard, wind-blown snow. The wind raged and threatened to blow us back the way we had come, a bitterly cold wind that soon numbed exposed skin. It was good to take a brief respite behind the large summit cairn before dropping down on to the relatively sheltered south-eastern slopes.

We made our way back to the Allt a' Chaorainn by way of an old tin bothy, where we sat and ate our piece. A hundred yards away a herd of stags muzzled below the blanket of snow in search of food, completely unconcerned with our presence.

Behind us a great rainbow was formed by the flying ice particles, and the sky beyond was a deep-blue. Away to the south, the sinking sun lit up a million-and-one lochans; the whole scene was as if someone had dropped glittering diamonds across the length and breadth of the country.

Grouse chattered and constantly told us to *go-back*, *go-back*, *go-back*, and blue hares scuttered away from almost beneath our feet. It was good to be up there in the early gloaming, good to share the kindness of the day through the savagery of the wind, good to realise that even in an area claimed by so many to be inferior, there is a hill that can surprise and please, that can offer challenge, and satisfy the urge to be in high places.

Coire Garbhlach

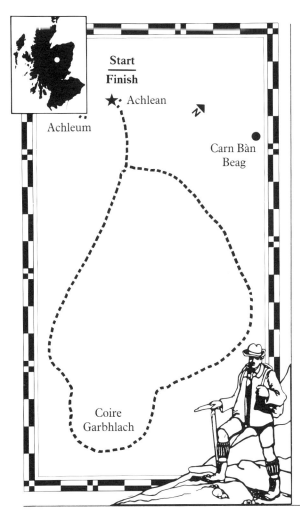

MAP: Ordnance Survey Sheet 36.

DISTANCE: Eight miles.

ASCENT: 2,000 ft.

DIFFICULTIES: An easy half-day walk, but could be spread into a full day walk by spending more time on the Great Moss, the Moine Mhor. The ascent out of Coire Garbhlach is steep.

ACCOMMODATION: Youth hostels at Kingussie and Aviemore. Private hostel at Ballochcroick in Glen Feshie. Hotels, guest-houses and bed-and-breakfast at Kincraig, Kingussie, Newtonmore and Aviemore.

I'm always amazed that folk who seem fairly familiar with the Cairngorms are often unaware of the existence of Coire Garbhlach. In its own way, it's as much of a gem as some of the more popular Cairngorm spots, yet it's comparatively unknown.

Winding into the Moine Mhor massif from Glen Feshie for about one-and-a-half miles, Coire Garbhlach is probably unique in the Cairngorms. Most corries are of the hanging-coire type, but Garbhlach is more of a long V-shaped glen, with steep, rugged flanks and a roaring stream in its floor.

I took a friend there fairly recently, a lad who's familiar with the Ciarngorms, but who knew nothing about Garbhlach. I could sense his surprise as we approached the glen from Achlean in Glen Feshie. We took the start of the

Foxhunter's Path, which eventually climbs high on to the Great Moss, near Carn Ban Mor, but soon after crossing the stile into the Cairngorms National Nature Reserve, we left the path for a delightful stroll through the old pine woods of Badan Mosach.

On the other side of the woods, a faint path through deep heather took us along some ancient glacial morraines until we saw the entrance of Coire Garbhlach before us. Soon we were following the path inside the corrie, each corner opening up another stretch of steep, craggy mountainside.

Half-way up the corrie, or the glen as it really is, a stream drops down a deep chasm, forming a spectacular waterfall. Either side of the fall was fringed with icicles, and the pool at the bottom was beginning to freeze at its edges. Little did we know then that higher up ice was almost going to bar our further progress.

We ate our lunch by the waterfall, watching a dipper further down the stream. A familiar sound made us both look up in surprise as a solitary snow-bunting passed us, carried along on the breeze. A small parcel of hinds stood on the hillside higher up the glen, with several stags of all ages watching us on the other side. We most certainly weren't alone.

Originally we had intended walking up the corrie to its end and returning the same way, but I had a notion to climb out the headwall of the corrie, traverse across the Moine Mhor to Carn

Ban Mor, and return to Achlean by the Foxhunter's Path. Steep snow-gullies in the corrie's headwall looked attractive, though, and we couldn't resist the temptation. A good snow-scramble's always enjoyable.

We both carried walkers' ice-axes, so we knew that if we did slip we could arrest the slide easily enough. I was more concerned about the snow slipping away, as much of the gully floor was made of snow which had been deposited by the wind. But it seemed solid enough, and we reckoned we could give it a go.

All went well until near the top, when the snow both steepened and turned to ice. I had no idea it had been so cold, and suddenly the snow was too hard to kick our boots into. Further to our right, the stream, which normally comes crashing down from the edge of the Moine Mhor, had frozen up, and the rocky buttress over which it normally flows had became a great, icy crag, green in the dull light. It looked impressive, and we realised that we most certainly couldn't get out of the corrie in that direction, certainly not without crampons on our boots.

It looked as though our only choice would be to retreat; back down the snow gully and back to Glen Feshie the way we had come. But as we made faltering steps back down the ice, I noticed a short subsidiary gully easing off to the left. Some rocks had formed a ramp, and the snow which had fallen there hadn't frozen. I made my way across the ice to it, gingerly hanging on to my single axe placement. Fortunately, there was little ice on the rocks, and with a mixture of rock-scrambling and kicking steps in the softer snow, we managed to make our way to the harder, less-steep snow which led on to the plateau.

CLIMBING OUT of the confines of Coire Garblach, in the Cairngorms. As you climb out onto the wide open slopes of the Moine Mhor, the Great Moss it is like entering another world, particularly in winter time.

It's a long time since I've felt as cold as I did then. The wind which blew across the Great Moss was icy, and I realised how the ice had formed so quickly on Coire Garbhlach's headwall. The walk across to Carn Ban Mor became a battle into the teeth of a gale. Winter had arrived, and with a vengeance.

In normal summer conditions this walk is a joy, exciting from the corrie at its head on to the strange, flat plateau of the Moine Mor, the Great Moss. It's always a treat to wander across this high place, with the lonely sound of golden plover to keep you company. Head back to Glen Feshie from the shallow col east of Carn Ban Mor, and follow the Foxhunter's Path back to Achlean.

SLIOCH FROM the south east near Kinlochewe. At the start of the Slioch walk. The initial stages of the walk follow the river through some old woods. When you reach the shores of Loch Maree you have to start climbing northwards.

THE TORRIDON peaks from Slioch in late afternoon. There is something about this time of day which is always atmospheric. There is always a mental struggle between hanging around to enjoy this 'gloaming', or heading off the hill to beat the dark.

COIRE NAN Caime, Liathach. Looking west along the summit ridge to Mullach an Rathain. The traverse of Liathach makes a superb walk with some interesting scrambles over the Am Fasarinen Pinnacles. These difficulties can be avoided by a narrow path on the south.

FROM THE summit of Beinn Alligin looking towards the Horns of Alligin, Beinn Dearg, and the other peaks of the Flowerdale Forest. This is one of the remarkable landscape areas in Scotland. There is simply nowhere else quite like it.

THE CLASSIC view of Ben Nevis from Corpach. While Ben Nevis, the highest mountain in Britain, lacks the jagged outline of the Cuillin or the sheer splendour of An Teallach its size and bulk are breathtaking and there is no doubting that this is a mighty mountain indeed.

Rothiemurchus and Loch An Eilean, Badenoch

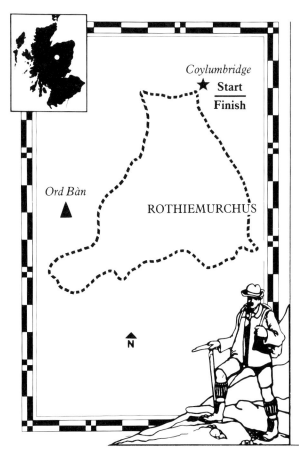

MAP: Ordnance Survey Sheet 36.

DISTANCE: Eight miles.

ASCENT: Low-level walk.

DIFFICULTIES: Nil.

ACCOMMODATION: Hotels, guest-houses, bed-and-breakfast in Aviemore, Kingussie, Newtonmore, Boat of Garten and Carrbridge. Youth hostels at Aviemore and Loch Morleich. Camp-sites at Coylumbridge and Glenmore.

Not all that long ago, much of the area that we nowadays know as the Scottish Highlands was densely covered by forest. Wolves, bears, elks and lynx roamed the hillsides; beavers swam in the lochs and larger rivers and, just as today, the golden eagle ruled the sky.

But *Homo sapiens* were quick to realise that these vast forests of Caledonian pine, birch and juniper not only gave shelter to wild animals, but to vagabonds and outlaws as well. There was also a need for timber, particularly to build ships, and the pines were felled. As the forests died, so did many of the wild animals. The wolves, bears, boars and many other species became extinct in Scotland, and the red deer, once a native forest-dweller, took to the hills.

Today, only remnants are left of that once-great forest. By far the finest is the great forest of Rothiemurchus, near Aviemore.

From the foot of the northern corries of the Cairngorm Mountains, a great plain runs in a north-westerly direction towards the River Spey and the Monadhliath Hills. Much of this plain is densely forested, the upper reaches in Glenmore by the modern conifers of the Forestry Commission, the lower reaches, in contrast, traditionally garbed. The natural red Scots pines of the Great Forest of Caledon are comparatively well spaced, with an abundant undergrowth of juniper and birch scrub.

The richness of the vegetation offers a good haunt for wildlife. Roe deer, red squirrel, otters and possibly even pine marten can be seen, and the bird-life is just as varied. Here you'll find birds of the titmouse family, the great tit, the blue-tit, the long-tailed tit and the rare crested tit. Crossbills feed on the abundant pine cones, and you're likely to spot siskin, lesser repolls, capercailles, and perhaps even an osprey fishing on Loch an Eilean.

Rothiemurchus is said to mean Fort of Muircas, from the Gaelic Rata-Mhurchuis, but who this Muircas was no-one seems to know. The most popular walk in the area is round Loch an

Eilean, the real jewel of Rothiemurchus and a loch with one of the loveliest settings in Scotland.

Begin at Coylumbridge, about one-and-a-half miles south-east of Aviemore on the Cairngorm road. Just before you reach the bridge over the Allt Druie, you'll see a sign on the right-hand side of the road which indicates the direction of the Lairig Ghru, the 30-mile pass which cuts through the heart of the Cairngorms to Braemar in the south. There is a parking lay-bye here, and with our walk finishing only half-a-mile back down the road, this route is virtually circular.

Follow the Lairig path through the woods. Soon you'll come to a split in the path beside a large cairn. Bear left, across a large meadow with some luxuriant juniper bushes on your right. Cross a stile and continue through the forest. After a while the Caledonian pines give way to the familiar conifers, close-planted and somehow lacking the character of the native trees.

SCATTERED LOCHS

As you leave the commercial forest, you come to a divergence in the ways. A path runs off to the right, towards your destination, Loch an Eilean. The route now runs westwards over an undulating moorland of heather and pine. Small lochans scattered here and there are usually inhabited by mallard and sometimes goldeneye duck. To the left the hills begin to rise from the heather moorland, the beginnings of the long Sgorans Ridge, which culminates in the Moine Mor above Glen Feshie.

This track is an ancient one, once known as the Rathad nam Mearlach, or the Caterans Road. In the sixteenth century, clansmen from the west would often take this road to the rich pasturelands of Morayshire, where they would steal the cattle and return westwards with their booty. This was the old road they used.

Soon you'll see the waters of Loch an Eilean sparkling through the trees, and again, you'll have a choice of route. You can turn right and follow the track to the car-park at the foot of Loch an Eilean, and so miss out the walk around the loch. Going round the loch adds three miles to the walk, but is well worth it. It's a glorious wander around one of Scotland's finest lochs, and I strongly recommend it. You can't get lost, for the track hugs the lochside for most of the way.

LOCAL LEGENDS

As you come close to the end of the walk round the loch, you'll notice the remains of a castle on an island in the loch, 50 yards or so from the shore. The building dates from about the fourteenth century, and some local legends have it that this was a keep belonging to the Wolf of Badenoch, one Alexander Stewart, the bastard son of Robert II of Scotland. Modern historians think this unlikely, but it's an interesting castle anyway. More recently the castle ruins were used by one of the last ospreys in Scotland before they became extinct early this century. The ospreys are, of course, back in Scotland, breeding successfully, and it would be nice to think that perhaps one day a pair will again breed successfully on the Loch an Eilean castle ruins.

At the foot of the loch is an information centre run by Rothiemurchus estate, and a car-park. Leave the car-park by the bridge that runs over the stream, follow the road for a 100 yards or so, and then turn right. Follow this track past some houses to the public road at Blackpark. Continue down the road to Inverdruie, and from there turn right on the Cairngorm road, back to your car at Coylumbridge.

Meall A'Bhuachaille

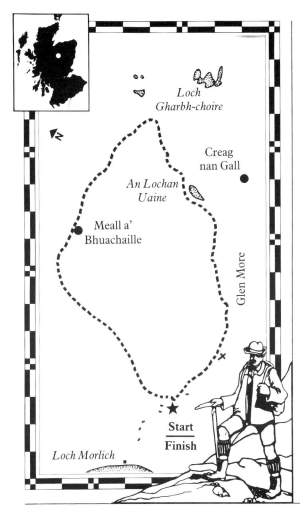

Loch Gharbh-choire

Creag nan Gall

An Lochan Uaine

Meall a' Bhuachaille

Glen More

Loch Morlich

Start
Finish

MAP: Ordnance Survey Sheet 36.

DISTANCE: Five miles.

ASCENT: 1,500 ft.

DIFFICULTIES: An easy and enjoyable half-day walk. Good views from the summit of Meall a'Bhuachaille.

ACCOMMODATION: Youth hostels at Loch Morlich and Aviemore. Hotels, guest-houses and bed-and-breakfast at Aviemore, Kingussie, Newtonmore, Carrbridge, Boat of Garten and Nethybridge. Camp-sites at Loch Morlich and Coylumbridge.

It's odd how you often get a better viewpoint from a wee hill than from some of its bigger neighbours. Meall a'Bhuachaille of Glenmore isn't exactly diminutive, but compared with its neighbours in the Cairngorms, it's a dumpy wee thing, the culmination point of a broad and long heathery ridge that runs up to Glenmore from Pityoulish.

But despite its lowly station, Meall a'Bhuachaille, the Hill of the Shepherd, is magnificently positioned. Right up at the head of Glenmore, forming one of the boundary walls of the Pass of Ryvoan, you can gaze from the summit all the way down the length of Glenmore and into Badenoch, all the way to the Laggan Hills and beyond.

Closer at hand, the great Northern Corries of the Cairngorms are seen from an unusual angle, with Cairngorm itself showing a more shapely and interesting outline than it does from Aviemore. Indeed a fine walk to Cairngorm can be traced from Meall a'Bhuachaille, up from Lochan Uaine, the Green Lochan, in the Pass of Ryvoan, and on to the Stranger's Crag, Creag nan gall. Follow the ridge to Stac na h-Iolaire, the Peak of the Eagle, and then follow the finely curving ridge to Cnap Coire na Spreidhe and Cairngorm itself.

But back to the Hill of the Shepherd . . . A track runs up the hill from Ryvoan Bothy, easily reached by the Forestry track that starts just past Glenmore Lodge, the National Mountaineering Centre in Glenmore. The path runs through the Pass of Ryvoan, past the Green Lochan, Lochan Uaine, so-named because local legend claims that the faery folk wash their clothes in the water. From the lochan, you can clearly see the gable end of Ryvoan Bothy in the distance.

From the bothy, the track runs up through the heather and begins quite a long and steady pull on to the Meall a'Buachaille ridge. As you climb, so the view becomes better, down on to the broad moorlands that sweep up towards Bynack Mor and Strathnethy to the saddle overlooking Loch Avon.

It's marvellous to think that the area below was once the starting point for cattle thieves beginning their long journey back to the confines of the western glens after raids on the rich and fertile lands of Moray. After the openness of the broad Moray plains, it must have been a welcome sight to see the narrow jaws of Ryvoan Pass, the jaws that swallowed them into obscurity as they melted into the byeways and secret ways to the west. The Caterans Road or Rath nan Mearlach.

From the summit of the hill a good path runs down to the *bealach* between Meal a'Bealach and Creagan Gorm. Turn left here and drop down into The Queen's Forest for a pleasant walk back through the wood to Glenmore.

THE WEST end of Loch Avon – 'the waters of A'an they rin sae clear, wad beguile a man for a hunner years'

Loch Avon and Beinn Mheadhoin

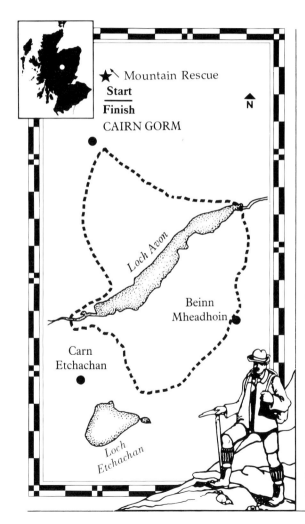

MAP: Ordnance Survey Sheet 36.

DISTANCE: 10 miles.

ASCENT: 3,300 ft.

DIFFICULTIES: A good introduction to Cairngorm walking. A long undertaking in winter, but shouldn't present any real difficulties for the strong walker in summer. Weather conditions can change suddenly in the Cairngorms though, and it's always good to bear in mind that escape routes involve either a climb back over the high and exposed Cairngorm Plateau or a long, long walk out via the Saddle and Strathnethy.

ACCOMMODATION: Youth hostels at Loch Morlich and Aviemore. Hotels, guest-houses and bed-and-breakfast at Aviemore, Kingussie, Newtonmore, Carrbridge, Boat of Garten and Nethybridge. Camp-sites at Loch Morlich and Coylumbridge.

In many ways the Cairngorms are peculiar mountains. Gaze at them from Speyside in the north, or from Braemar in the south, and they appear as high, rounded hills, pleasant enough but lacking the drama of the Cuillin of Skye or the giants of Torridon. The Cairngorms offer a completely different perspective. To appreciate these hills, you must get into them, for their real delights are well hidden from those who lack the motivation to climb them.

These hill also have a spaciousness that is unique. The skies are wider, the horizons more distant; these hills are bigger than anything else in these islands, with more land higher than 2,000 ft, 3,000 ft and 4,000 ft than any other mountain range in Britain.

This walk, I believe, offers the first-time visitor to the Cairngorms an opportunity to experience some of the special attributes of the area: the wide plateau, the deeply-cut chasms and corries, and Loch Avon, the real jewel of the Grampians.

Drive up Cairngorm to the Cairngorm chairlift car-park. You can either pay your money and take the chairlift to the top of Cairngorm or, if you have the time, walk up the Fiascaill Coire Cas, the obvious ridge that bounds the west side of the Coire Cas ski-grounds.

A large cairn sits at the top of the ridge, announcing the fact that here on in is National Nature Reserve. Head south, downhill over the plateau to Coire Raibert, your descent route to Loch Avon. The path begins to steepen quite abruptly and is very loose in places, so take care.

Below you the blue waters of Loch Avon soon come into sight, its edges tinged golden. There's an old saying that 'the waters of A'an they rin sae clear, wad beguile a man for a hunner years'. The water is indeed clear, and the loch immensely beautiful. As you reach the foot of Coire Raibert, you'll soon realise the immensity and granduer of its setting.

With the slopes of Cairngorm rising steeply on one side from the buttresses and clefts of the Stag Rocks, and the steep slopes of Beinn Meadhoin

A FROZEN Loch Avon and the massive crags of Creag Etchachan and the Shelterstone Crag. There is a wonderful atmosphere down here with high crags all around you. It's claimed that Loch Avon is haunted by a water horse, or kelpie.

rising almost sheer on the other side, Loch Avon is wedged tightly between the two. Directly ahead, another coire opens out – Coire Etchachan, separating the slopes of Beinn Meadhoin from the dark crags of Creag a Choire Etchachan. Further right an enormous square-cut block of rock dominates the scene. This is the Sticil or, as it is commonly known, the Shelter Stone Crag, one of the most impressive natural features in the area. Below it, amid a tumble of scree rocks and boulders, some the size of a double-decker bus, is the well-known 'howff' of Shelter Stone, a cavern below a gigantic rock, big enough to take several walkers in comfort.

You'll see the Shelter Stone easily enough from the end of Loch Avon, but your route climbs up and out of the loch's basin, up the obvious path that leads to Coire Etchachan and its loch.

This spot is pure Arctic. Loch Etchachan caresses the 3,000 ft contour and in some years is completely free from ice for only four or five months. Beyond it the crags lead to the slopes of Ben MacDhui, the second-highest mountain in Britain, and to the south, a broad ridge that leads to Derry Cairngorm.

Views of Loch Etchachan expand as you leave the track and climb the slopes of Beinn Meadhoin to its strange granite summit tors. The tallest is about 25 ft high, a mini-crag in red granite. A cleft on the northern side offers an easy scramble to the top. These tors consist of granite bedrock more solid and more resistant to weathering than the surrounding ground. It's believed that they were formed when the climate was both warmer and wetter than it is now, after the time when the whole of this massif was submerged under the ice which carved out the deep glens.

And it's to the deep glen that we return, down the rough northern slopes to the foot of Loch Avon, where the River Avon begins it's long journey to its confluence with the Spey. You'll be able to cross quite easily here before beginning the long climb to the Saddle which separates Loch Avon from the start of Strathnethy. Above, the long slopes of Cairngorm look steep and high at the end of the day, but it's never as hard as it looks. The long pull takes you up on to Cairngorm by Ciste Mhearhaid and then over into the Ptarmigan Corrie, from where you can follow the ski roads back to the car-park.

Braeriach, Badenoch

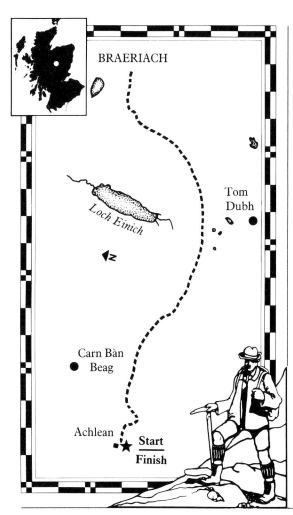

BRAERIACH

Loch Einich

Tom Dubh

Carn Bàn Beag

Achlean

Start

Finish

MAP: Ordnance Survey Sheet 36.

DISTANCE: 15 miles.

ASCENT: 3,200 ft.

DIFFICULTIES: A straightforward, if long, high-level walk. Navigation could be difficult in low visibility, as much of the walking is above the 3,000 ft contour. Choose a good, clear day if possible. A long and serious undertaking in winter.

ACCOMMODATION: Youth hostels at Kingussie and Aviemore. Private hostel at Ballachcroick in Glen Feshie. Hotels, guest-houses and bed-and-breakfast at Kincraig, Kingussie, Newtonmore and Aviemore.

When I'm asked which is my favourite Cairngorm mountain, I give a swift answer: Braeriach, the Brindled Upland, Britain's third-highest hill and the Cairngorm's second-highest.

When that reply is followed by another question – 'Why?' – I take a little longer to answer. Look at Braeriach from Speyside and see it rise in a squat crouch behind the sharp cone of little Carn Elrig, a massive bulk of a hill, its summit thrown up by the highest points of no fewer than five corries, all steep and and craggy and magnificent.

But climb the hill from Achlean, in Glen Feshie, up the Foxhunter's Track to Carn Ban Mor, across the Great Moss or the Moine Mor, and up those long north-western slopes to the summit cairn to gaze down the long, empty miles of Glen Dee, and you will begin to understand its claim to be the best of the Cairngorms.

Across the chasm that is is An Garbh Coire, the twin peaks of Cairn Toul and Sgurr an Lochain Uaine rise in a long sweep from the screes and ochreous corrie floor, both peaks sheltering the lonely waters of Lochan Uaine, a textbook corrie lochan. Across the Lairig Ghru, the edge of the Cairngorm/Ben MacDhui plateau suddenly stops, and over the edge pour the foaming waters of the March Burn and the Tailor's Burn, long, grey mares' tails in the summer and invisible in winter as all is under the great white shroud that stifles and muffles the sound of the ptarmigan.

To be up here on the edge of five corries, is like standing atop a western peak, a *sgurr* rather than a *meall*, a *stac* as opposed to a *monadh*.

SPRING AVALANCHES

But memories, too, score points in the choosing of favourites, and I recall with fondness the traverse I made of the hill some years ago, sleeping out in the mild spring evenings, and traversing all five corries, climbing on narrow ridges and watching spring avalanches in Coire an Lochain. I recall, too, the night I spent not far from the summit, watching the antics of a pair of dotterel before sleeping with my head against the summit cairn. I was wakened early in the morning by one of the finest sounds of the high tops; the summer song of the cock snow-bunting. If ever

CAIRN TOUL and Sgurr an Lochan Uaine from Braeriach. A very fine high level traverse takes you round the very edge of the Braeriach plateau to Sgurr an Lochain Uaine, the Peak of the Green Corrie to Cairn Toul, the Hill of the barn.

Looking up the length of the Lairig Ghru with Ben MacDhui on the left and the slopes of Sron na Lairig and Braeriach on the right. The Lairig Ghru is one of the classic through routes of the highlands.

there was a song full of the joy of life, it is this. Up he soars high in the air, like a skylark, before sailing back to earth in a crescendo of shattering bird-song.

Alarmingly, too, Braeriach ranks favourite among those who covet innaccessible mountains for ski-development. This great hill holds snow longer and better than any other in the country, but that is no justification for despoiling it. You can ski it now when the snow in Coire Gorm is at its finest, but you must pay the not unreasonable price of having to carry in your skis by Shank's Pony.

Bibliography

TECHNICAL BOOKS

Barton, Bob, *A Chance in a Million*, (SMT 1985). A book on Scottish avalanches, includes case histories.

British Mountaineering Council, *Mountain Hypothermia*, (BMC 1972). Concise leaflet.

Cliff, Peter, *Mountain Navigation*, (Cordee, 1986). Very fine paperback on navigation techniques.

Langmuir, Eric, *Mountaincraft and Leadership*, (Scottish Sports Council 1984). Very fine handbook for anyone going onto Scottish hills.

Pedgley, David, *Mountain Weather*, (Cicerone Press, 1979). Practical paperback guide to weather conditions most often met in the hills.

Renouf, J and Hulse S, *First Aid for Hillwalkers*, (Cicerone Press, 1982). First class paperback.

GENERAL BOOKS

Butterfield, Irvine, *The High Mountains of Britain and Ireland*, (Diadem, 1986). Beautifully illustrated guidebook to the hills of Britain. Suggested itineries and good advice. A coffee table type book.

Gilbert, Richard, *Big Walks, Classic Walks and Wild Walks*, (Diadam Books) Three marvellous books which are well written and superbly illustrated.

McNeish, Cameron and Smith, Roger, *Classic Walks in Scotland*, (Oxford Illustrated Press 1988). High level and low level walks throughout Scotland.

McNeish, Cameron, *Backpacker's Scotland*, (Robert Hale 1982). Long distance treks throughout Scotland.

McNeish, Cameron, *Backpacker's Manual*, (Oxford Illustrated Press 1984). Handbook on walking and lightweight camping techniques and skills.

Poucher, Walt, *Scottish Peaks*, (Constable 1965). Photo illustrated guide to walks in Scotland. Remarkable for its consistency of high quality photographs.

Scottish Mountaineering Trust, *The Munros*, (SMT 1985). A hardback colour guide to Scotland's 3000 ft mountains. A must for any Scottish hill walker.

Scottish Mountaineering Club, *District Guidebooks*, 76 volumes, (SMT). Illustrated hardback guides to all the mountain areas of Scotland.

Index